S0-BNB-000

MOBILIZING HUMAN RESOURCES

by Richard Pinder

PNEUMA LIFE
PUBLISHING

MOBILIZING HUMAN RESOURCES

Published by:

PUBLISHING

All Scripture quotations, unless noted otherwise, are from the Holy Bible, New International Version, Copyright © 1973, 1978 1984 International Bible Society. Used by permission of Zondervan Bible Publishers.

All rights reserved. No part of this book may be reproduced in any form without permission in writing from the publisher, except in the case of brief quotations embodied in church related publications, critical articles or reviews.

Quotations from the King James Version have been denoted (KJV).

Printed in the United States of America

Copyright ©1994
Richard Pinder
P.O. Box N-9583
Nassau, Bahamas

Mobilizing Human Resources
ISBN 1-56229-415-6
$7.95 Soft Cover

Pneuma Life Publishing
P.O. Box 10612
Bakersfield, CA 93389
(805) 837-2113

Contents

Dedication

Acknowledgments

Foreword

Preface

Introduction

Chapter   Page

Dedication

To my precious pearl, my wife, Sheena who is a true manifestation of God's love and an excellent example of a help mate. She has been a constant source of encouragement, support and inspiration. She has freed me to pursue my purpose in helping to mobilize the human resources in the Body of Christ.

To my two little blessings from the Lord, my son Richard Rinnah and daughter, Talia Marie who constantly remind me of the next generation of human resources in the Kingdom and the need for them to understand their importance to the Kingdom.

To the thousands who will be encouraged to find their place, utilize their abilities and in so doing exhibit the glory of God and establish the reality of the Kingdom of God on Earth.

Acknowledgement

This book is the result of many years of experience made possible by those who saw the potential in me and allowed me to utilize the gifts, talents and abilities which were placed inside of me from before I was in my mother's womb.

I am especially appreciative to the members and colleagues at Bahamas Faith Ministries Fellowship whose confidence, encouragement and prayerful support have motivated me to become all that God has designed me to be. I am thankful for their patience in allowing me to grow in my purpose. To Marian Sturrup and Beverley Dwyer for your willing and able assistance.

I am particularly grateful to the following persons:

My lovely wife Sheena and our children who have had to grow with me and the ministry and who have had tremendous patience when I could not be home with them because of my responsibilities in the ministry. Your support is vital.

My father, Richard H. Pinder II who, along with my deceased mother, Margaret gave me birth. Thank you daddy for your encouragement.

My deceased grand aunt, Marie Butler who the Lord provided to mother me and who, by her example, made it very easy for me to accept Christ as my Lord and Savior.

My pastor friend and brother-in-law, Myles Munroe.

Your encouragement and ability to recognize giftings and make room for them is truly God given. I appreciate you.

My very special friend and sister-in-law, Ruthann Munroe. Your quiet support and prayers are a rich source of strength.

My other close friends, pastors and board members: Henry and Sheila Francis, David and Angie Burrows, Wesley and Debbie Smith, Jay and Euterpia Mullings, Charles and Cassandra Nottage, Eme and Angie Achara, Noel and Gloria Seymour, Allan and Nyoka Munroe, Felix and Cyprianna Rolle, Theo and Blooming Neely whose encouragement and friendship have assisted me greatly in fulfilling my purpose.

My friends in ministry: Turnel Nelson, Bertril Baird, Peter Morgan, Fuchsia Pickett, Jerry Horner, Allan Langstaff, Kingsley Fletcher, Frank Seebransingh and many others too numerous to mention.

Lastly, but most importantly to the King of Kings and Lord of Lords, Jesus Christ, the Source of my existence and my Reason for being. He is the Sustainer of my life. The precious Paraclete, the Holy Spirit, my constant Guide and Discerner of all truth. Thanks for the joy of fulfilling my purpose.

To every member of the Kingdom of God who will begin to understand that they are vital and important to the Kingdom of God.

Foreword

The possession of a guiding purpose and vision is the source of true leadership. However, the ultimate test of leadership is the effective, efficient management of resources, both human and material. The sands of history are littered with remnants of great dreams, visions and ideas that failed because of the leader's lack of ability to execute the dream. Executive ability involves the uses of organizational, administrative and management skills. The need for these skills in all successful endeavors is crucial, especially in non-profit organizations like the Church where commitment, faithfulness and high morale is motivated by a sense of belonging and significance.

The need for excellence in organizational and management skills in the administration of the Church is mandatory, especially in our highly technical society, where so much is competing for the attention of the market. Many pastors and other leaders who have come out of highly, tightly structured denominational backgrounds were so organized and had to follow a format so rigorously, that now they are almost paranoid of formats. It is true we should not get so organized that the Holy Spirit is blocked from our endeavors, but it is equally true that proper organization will eliminate confusion and display quality and excellence in all we do to the Glory of God. After all He Himself does all things decently and orderly.

The Church, like our physical body, is an organization that needs to be organized to maximize its potential and to function efficiently and effectively. Organization is only a means to an end, not an end in itself. An organization is a social system deliberately established to carry out some definite purpose. It consists of a number of people in two pattern of relationships. The Biblical definition of an organization is recorded in 1 Cor. 12:12,14,18: "The body is a unit, though it is made up of many parts, and though all its parts are many, they form one body. So it is with Christ... Now the body is not made up of one part, but many...In fact God has arranged the parts in the body everyone of them just as he wanted them to be."

Every organization has work to do in the real world and there must be some way of measuring how well that work is done. It is the responsibility of leadership/management to see that the work gets done as efficiently and effectively as possible.

Effectiveness is doing the right thing. Efficiency is doing things right. In this book, "Mobilizing Human Resources," Richard Pinder presents a concise, Biblically sound approach to organizing Human Resources of Ministry Organization for maximum efficiency with a view to mobilizing the entire organization into a corporate team.

Richard uses his practical experience gained over many years of organizing, developing, training and managing the Personnel of Bahamas Faith Ministries International, to offer advice and insights into various challenges of organizations. Every minister, pastor and leader of any capacity of responsibility, would find this work a priceless asset to a more efficient and effective management of God's Kingdom Business.

Dr. Myles Munroe
Nassau, Bahamas

Preface

**"Our most precious resource on the planet is
not our oil wells, but the human resources."**

In Genesis 1:28, God said to Adam and Eve to be
fruitful, multiply and fill the earth. At the time this
command was given they had not sinned and so had not
fallen short of the glory of God. I believe God's intention
was to fill the earth with replicas of Himself - those who
bear His glory. In other words if they had reproduced after
their kind in their sinless state, the earth would have been
full of God's influence.

When Jesus was about to be received back into heaven
in Matt 28:18-20, the very same thought is expressed.
Just before His suffering, Jesus prayed the Father for the
church, "I have given them the glory that you gave me, that
they may be one as we are one" (John 17:22). This means
that the purpose of God never changed; God still wants the
earth to be full of Himself and He has chosen a medium
through which to do it.

The Church is the vehicle through which God intends
to reveal Himself to man and make disciples. The only way
men will know of the Kingdom of God is through the lives
of its citizens and through the ministry of Church. The
difficulty we have been facing is that the Church has not
been mobilized. The valuable human resources have not
reached their potential because we have not understood
the **Ministry of Helps.**

com/ng to the fellowship of believers assembled

The Ministry of Helps, in its simplest form, is the coordination and operation of every member of the Body of Christ toward the establishing of the Kingdom of God in the lives of men. It is when each member fulfills this goal and functions as a part of the Body of Christ as given him by the Head of the Body of Christ.

Until we understand that every member of the Body of Christ is unique with gifts, talents and abilities, we cannot fully tap into our most precious resource - the human resources or begin to fill the earth with the influence of the King of the Kingdom.

Growing up in the church and having had the opportunity over the past 22 years to be involved with churches, talking with pastors from varied backgrounds, I have concluded that many churches are stagnant or simply not reaching their maximum potential, because there is little, if any, understanding of the **Ministry of Helps** or **Ministerial Support Staff**.

In the chapters which follow, we will examine what the **Ministry of Helps** is and why we need to begin to mobilize our human resources to fill the earth with Himself. We will see how God has designed the Church to function in unity and unison so that the Kingdom of God can advance. You will be encouraged and motivated to fulfill your purpose in the Body of Christ.

Now let us examine together the plan and purpose of God as it relates to your importance and position in the Body of Christ.

Introduction

Everyone of us has experienced the debilitating effect of chaos. You may have opened the door of your teenager's bedroom and found clothing strewn all over the floor, and socks and shoes out of position. Our initial response is to want to close the door, yet we know that this same room, once organized, can be a beautiful picture of order and productivity.

Chaos is a very serious state because of the magnitude of its result. There are five basic effects of chaos:

(1) Helpless immobilization. If a situation is confusing, you feel immobilized and have no initiative to proceed.

(2) The feeling of a lack of purpose. Once you lose sight of purpose, your motivation and actions become ineffective.

(3) The lack of productivity.

(4) A wastage of precious resources and a limiting of potential.

(5) The end result of chaos is stagnation.

There is, however, a positive side to a chaotic situation; it at least gives you a reference point from which to begin.

If used correctly, confusion and disorganization can become the catalyst to order and productivity.

I believe God did this very thing in Genesis when He saw the earth as void and in a state of confusion. The first thing He did was to bring order, which in turn brought productivity and a fulfillment of purpose. Fulfillment of purpose is achieved once we understand our objectives, identify our resources and employ our potential.

God has placed an awesome potential and a rich resource in every human being. The purpose of that deposit is for the fulfillment of the vision for the Church.

Many Pastors have been discouraged because they did not see how confusion and lack of productivity could be turned into an encouraging success story.

Many laymen have been frustrated and disheartened because they were told they had nothing to contribute to the Kingdom of God, and only certain people had worth.

This book is designed to give you the foundation on which to begin to change your confusion into order, and your lack of productivity into a monument of success.

You will understand the difference between volunteerism and responsible productiveness. You will learn that you are a vital part of the Church, and your gifts and abilities are necessary to the fulfillment of the vision of your local Church.

Finally, in the last two chapters, you will find practical aid to organizing and managing precious human resources.

1

WHAT IS THE MINISTRY OF HELPS?

> Now about spiritual gifts, brothers, I do not want you to be ignorant. You know that when you were pagans, somehow or other you were influenced and led astray to mute idols. Therefore I tell you that no one who is speaking by the Spirit of God says, 'Jesus be cursed,' and no one can say, 'Jesus is Lord,' except by the Holy Spirit. There are <u>different kinds of gifts, but</u> the same Spirit. <u>There are different kinds of service</u>, but the same Lord. There are different kinds of working, but the same God works all of them in all men. Now to each one the manifestation of the Spirit is given for the common good. (I Corinthians 12:1-7)

As we seek to define the Ministry of Helps, I believe I Corinthians 12 is an excellent place to begin.

According to this passage, there are different gifts, but it is the same Spirit - Spirit of God. In other words, there should not be a situation in the church when the gifts are not operating, or where a person feels his gift is more important than another's.

There are people in the church who do not exercise self-control in their expression of the gifts. According to the Word of God, the Spirit of the prophet, is subject to the prophet (I Cor.14:32). How is that possible? Why should Paul not allow a free flow of gifts in the church? Because, the gifts operate through one Spirit, and God is a God of order not of disorder. For example, God did not create man, then later remembered that he needed oxygen to breathe. He created the oxygen first, then He was ready to create man. So we can look at Genesis and learn the lesson of order. In other words, God says, "I am going to give different gifts to different people in the church, but they are to operate in order for they are operating from the same Spirit.

What does this imply? If someone in the church is operating in a gift and causing confusion, he is out of order. Have you ever been in a service where one person stands up to give a word from the Lord, and another person jumps up right behind him, trying to drown him out? When God gives you a gift, it is to operate under authority to ensure order. This also ensures that the gift is maximized.

If one person is giving a word, and someone else jumps up with another word and thus makes it impossible to hear the message, the church is not benefiting from either word. God is after productivity and wants you to maximize your gift.

SERVE THE LORD, NOT MAN

Paul continues in verse 5 that there are different kinds of service, but it is the same Lord you're working for. God may give you the ability to serve by cleaning the facility. He may give somebody else the ability to serve by greeting at the door. Someone else may serve by operating the projector, but none is in the business of trying to figure out who is more important than the other. Why? Because it is one Lord everyone is serving and with a common goal of obeying the Head and moving the Body.

Some people come into the church seeking recognition and when they don't get it, they decide not to serve. They should bear in mind that it is not the pastor that they are serving but their Lord. The pastor does not impart gifts. If you are serving one Lord, there is no place for competition. There is no place for envy. There is place only for encouraging one another.

This is important because if I encourage my sister to be the best she can be in utilizing her gifts, and she is encouraging me to utilize mine to the best of my ability, both of us are going to be the best we can be and the church is going to move closer to the vision God has given the pastor.

Unfortunately, many times when we should be encouraging each other, we are busy tearing each other down while Satan stands on the outside and laughs on.

Think about this, if all members in your church were to function 100% in the gifts, talents and abilities God has given each one, wouldn't the church progress? The world would be frightened of us. You know why the world isn't frightened? Because we bring the mentality of the world into the church and operate just like them. We are jockeying for position. We want the pastor to notice us. We want to be in position where we can be seen and heard.

Verse 6 indicates that there are different kinds of "working." Now some people are fine until you use that word. In the church we are afraid to work and I don't understand why. It is very interesting that most of us have little difficulty reporting to our jobs, irrespective of the weather or physical condition. Yet, we offer excuses when we need to report to church and function in our ministerial staff positions.

BE FAITHFUL

I want you to see how insincere we sometimes can be. When it comes to the church and being responsible for what God has given us, some of us are not even found faithful. "I'm not going because I don't like the way the pastor spoke to me last night. He didn't call me up last week. I don't like the way that sister talks to people." I have news for you. There are some people on your job that speak to you in ways you don't appreciate. But you stand out in the cold to catch the bus to go to work and endure their behavior.

In the church, you are a part of something that is eternal. When you fulfill your "Ministry of Helps" position in the church, <u>you are fulfilling your purpose and establishing something that is going to last for eternity.</u>

We do not succeed in anything without work. If we are going to fill the earth with the influence of God, we must work and we have a lot to do. At Bahamas Faith Ministries, lazy people would be very uncomfortable. People there work because they understand that they are working for the Kingdom. The reason some of you haven't been working like you should is that you don't understand why we work and for Whom we work. Do not think you are working for the pastor.

I always tell people, it would have been so nice if God had given us angels for pastors. <u>But He gives us men, human beings with human frailties, with human weaknesses.</u> Were He to send us angels, there wouldn't be any fault for you to see. You could feel good about him all the time.

Yet, God has always worked through men and women. Why? The earth belongs to us. In the Old Testament, all He used angels for was to carry messages, but man had to do the work. It would have been nice if He'd sent an angel to deliver the children of Israel out of Egypt but He sent Moses. God will always use men and women.

✳ The faults the leader has are between him and his Maker. The pastor is on assignment and he is responsible to his Boss, and that's not you. It is God. A lot of people get confused and think that the pastor is working for them. He is working for God. It is God to whom he has to answer at the end of the day.

YOUR GIFTS ARE FOR THE GOOD OF OTHERS

Paul says in verses 6 and 7, *"There are different kinds of working but the same God works all of them in all men. Now to each one the manifestation of the Spirit is given for the common good."* So all of these gifts, all of these workings, all of these services, are given for what? They are given, "for the common good."

What makes up that word "common?" What other word do we get from that? Communion. Community. What does that imply? Common union. All that God places in the body is for everybody's good, not just yours. What you have is not just for your benefit.

If what God gave you is not just for you, then you have a responsibility to share it with the people for whom He gave it to you. You cannot sit home because you do not feel like using your gift. You are robbing the people for whom God gave you the gift and you are misusing your gift. This is called "gift abuse."

These gifts are given for the community's good. These are given for the good of the Body so that we may be linked with one another. What God has given you is to link us with what He has given the next person and the person after that and so on. When everyone links up, the Body starts to move. This is what **helps** is all about. And every time the Body moves, the earth is a little more full of His purpose and glory. This is God's original purpose.

As a result of our unwillingness to work and use our gifts, there has been a lot of church or Body neglect. God has given us what the rest of the Body needs and if we sit home and decide, "I'm not giving it." That is neglect.

In verse 8, Paul says, *"To one there is given through the Spirit the message of wisdom, to another the message of knowledge by means of the same Spirit, to another faith by the same Spirit, to another gifts of healing by that one Spirit, to another miraculous powers, to another prophecy, to another the ability to distinguish between spirits, to another the ability to speak in different kinds of tongues and to still another the interpretation of tongues. All these are the work of one and the same Spirit. And He gives them to each one just as He determines."* God gives gifts just as He determines.

If God had left it to us, in our finite wisdom, most of us would have chosen gifts that we couldn't handle. For example, some people want to preach and we know they can't preach. When God created us, He put in the blueprints everything that we need to function. At the same time that He put inside of you talents, gifts and abilities, He also gave you everything needed to maximize them. But, if you step outside of what He has given you, you are not equipped or authorized to operate in another gift.

Most of you have a driver's license. But if you were to step inside a tractor, could you handle it? Probably not. Your driver's license did not equip you to handle a tractor, it equipped you to handle a car.

Do you understand why there has been so much abuse in the church? First of all, people have been trying to operate in gifts they don't have. This often shows up in people who want to sing. For some reason I don't understand, singing is very attractive to people. They come up to you and say, "Pastor, I want to sing." But I now they just can't sing. People come up and they try to talk the pastor into letting them do something they're not equipped to do.

That is like you going to the heavy equipment company saying, "Sir, I have a driver's license here. It is valid and I have been driving for ten years and I want to drive this tractor." The man looks at you and shakes his head. There are people who do the very same thing in the church. They act in gifts they don't have forgetting that God is the One who gives, just as He determines.

WE ARE ACCOUNTABLE TO GOD

When you begin to understand your responsibility in the "Ministry of Helps," you begin to realize that you have to function because <u>you are accountable to God</u>. This has nothing to do with the pastor. The pastor is just the overseer and the administrator, but God is the One who gives the gifts, just as He wills.

Do you realize that when God created man, He did not create man for Satan? Everything that you have, everything that you are, everything that God put into you, He put it there for Himself. <u>Every ability you have came from God</u>. Satan didn't give you anything, and God didn't give it to you for Satan. Therefore, everything He has given you, He is holding you accountable for.

Now the good part of being held accountable is this: God is going to reward you when you do it. If you are a good steward of what He has given you, He is going to reward you.

One day I was driving along and I was a little discouraged. Then the Lord said to me, "Listen, I've got news for you. Nobody else is going to get your reward." That might not mean much to you, but that made me shout. God said to me, "Relax, you've been faithful. Nobody's going to steal your reward. That has your name on it."

See, you may be a little discouraged at times and disappointed by the behavior of people, but be encouraged because God doesn't miss a thing. He takes note of everything that you do. He doesn't slumber nor sleep. He will reward you according to your faithfulness. When we understand this, we begin to realize that our accountability is not to man, but to God. When you understand this Scriptural truth, you report for duty in the church with joy.

> **For You created my inner most being. You knit me together in my mother's womb. I praise You because I am fearfully and wonderfully made; Your works are wonderful. I know that full well. My frame was not hidden from You when I was made in the secret place, when I was woven together in the depths of the Earth, where I saw my unformed body. All the days ordained for me were written in Your book before one of them came to be.** Psalms 139:13

Before you were born, before your parents even thought about you, God already had a book written about you. Now, who determines whether you fulfill what's in that book? It can't be God for He already wrote it. It has to be you. When you begin to understand this, you report for duty with joy.

Wherever God sets you in the Body of Christ, whichever church He sets you in, you submit yourself to the authority with joy. Why? Because you're not here by accident. It doesn't matter what the circumstances of your birth were. His book about you is for your good and your success. God has a book for everyone to fulfill but each person determines the outcome. Don't waste your life trying to fulfill somebody else's purpose.

I want you to understand the implications of this truth. You can't go to God and say, "God, I can't do that." God is going to say, "Wait a minute, what are you saying? I made you. I put inside of you everything you need to fulfill your purpose, what do you mean you can't?"

What God has put into you comes out of you under pressure and is matured with use. God gives you leadership to motivate you. <u>The people who motivate themselves are called leaders.</u> Everybody else has to be motivated from outside. So, when you begin to realize that God has a purpose for you, you realize you have a responsibility before God to fulfill it, and to be responsible with what He has given you.

You have to think like God if you want to fulfill your purpose, and you'll find that you are so busy doing so, that you don't have time to worry about anyone else. You don't have time to look at your neighbor and say, "Well, she isn't doing this and she isn't doing that..." You are so busy trying to fulfill your own purpose that you won't have time to look over and envy somebody else and say, "Well, look at that, he has that talent and I don't have that and I only have..." You better get busy. You are wasting time.

The Bible says to whom much is given, much is required. If you see people who have ten talents, don't envy them. They have a lot of work to do. They have a lot of responsibility. One day God is going to ask them, "What did you do with all of this?" When you start to get this revelation, you'll start to thank God you don't have some gifts.

The approach you have been taking all the time was one of envy. You might start saying, "Thank God I don't have that." And you will realize that what you have, will take you a lifetime to do. Why burden yourself with somebody else's gifts? You only have one lifetime.

PRINCIPLES

1. God is a God of order.

2. Although there are different gifts, they come from the same Spirit.

3. When you fulfill your "Ministry of Helps" position in the church, you are fulfilling your purpose and establishing something that is going to last for eternity.

4. We do not succeed in anything without work.

5. God has always worked through men, because the earth belongs to us.

6. What you have is not for you, your gifts are given for the community good.

7. Everything God has given you, He holds you accountable for.

8. What God has put into you is what comes out of you under pressure, and is matured with use.

9. God gives you leadership to motivate you.

2

BENEFITS OF THE MINISTRY OF HELPS

When the Bible says we perish, it is not for lack of good will, nor for lack of good intentions, but <u>people perish for lack of knowledge</u>. You may have good intentions but without knowledge you will perish. Paul addresses the church at Corinth concerning this lack of knowledge.

Now about spiritual gifts brothers, I do not want you to be ignorant. You know that when you were pagans, somehow or other you were influenced and led astray to mute idols. I Cor. 12:1,2

All of us are led by something, some by their desires, some by habits, others by a bad relationship, etc. If it is something other than the Spirit, God calls it a "dumb idol."

Therefore I tell you that no one who's speaking by the Spirit of God says, 'Jesus be accursed.' And no one can say, 'Jesus is Lord.' except by the Holy Spirit. There are different kinds of gifts, but the same Spirit. There are different kinds of service, but they have the same Lord. There are different kinds of working, but the same God works all of

them in all men. Now, to each one the manifestation of the Spirit is given for the common good. I Cor. 12:3-7

As stated earlier, a principle is everything God has given us for the common good. It is also for other people's benefit, not just for yourself. Every gift God gives, every talent He gives is not for you, but for the Body, so that the members can minister to one another. God makes it very clear that everything that has been given is for the common good of the whole Body.

To one there is given, through the Spirit, the message of wisdom. To another the message of knowledge, by means of the same Spirit. To another, faith by the same Spirit. To another, gifts of healing by that one Spirit. To another miraculous powers; to another prophecy; to another the ability to distinguish between spirits; to another the ability to speak in different kinds of tongues. And to still another the interpretation of tongues. All these are the work of one and the same Spirit. And he gives them to each one just as he determines. I Cor. 12:8-11

GOD GIVES GIFTS, NOT MAN

Another principle is that God gives these gifts as He wills, not as we will. So God reserves the right to decide whom He will give what to. You might say, "Why give that to her? Why give it to him? Why not give it to me?" But God reserves the right to decide whom He will give what gift to. You don't have a vote in it. There is no democracy involved in this deal. God determines just as He wills, and He gives as He determines.

Paul moves into verse 12 using the human body as an analogy of the Body of Christ:

Verse 12: "The body is a unit. Though it is made up of many parts, and though all of its parts are many, they form one body. So it is with Christ."

Verse 13: "For we were all baptized by one Spirit into one body, whether Jews or Greeks, slave or free, and we were all given the one Spirit to drink."

In other words, in the Body of Christ, ethnic background, economic status, family background, make no difference in the Kingdom of God. God sees everybody the same. God sees everybody as either saved or unsaved. So God sees all of us equal in the church. Therefore He gives the gifts as He wills.

Verse 14: "Now the body is not made up of one part, but of many. If the foot should say, because I'm not a hand I do not belong to the body, it would not for that reason cease to be a part of the body. And if the ear should say because I'm not an eye, I do not belong to the body, it would not for that reason cease to be a part of the body.

If the whole body were an eye, where would the sense of hearing be? If the whole body were an ear, where would the sense of smell be? But, in fact, God has arranged the parts in the body."

Sometimes we are guilty of disputing God's arrangement, even trying to rearrange it. We say things like, "Well, God, I don't like brother B. In fact, I don't see why he has that gift. It should be given to brother J." We are trying to rearrange what God has already set into motion for His own purpose.

If you are going to be effective in the Body of Christ, it is important to note that once God decides what gifts He will give you, you must begin to function in them. It's like the ear wanting to be the eye. It doesn't matter how much it wants to see, it cannot. It must perform its original function if it is to be effective.

Verse 24: "While our presentable parts need no special treatment, God has combined the members of the body and has given greater honor to the parts that lacked it so that there should be no division in the body."

Note the word "division." *"So that there should be no division in the body."* In other words, the minute your physical body starts to fight against itself, you are in trouble. Your body was designed to heal itself and to work for its own benefit.

If your brain refuses to send any signal to your eyes to open so you can see, you are in trouble. You just turn blind. Think about it. So also in the Body of Christ, if you refuse to function in your duty, you have just hindered the progress of the Kingdom. What a sobering thought! You are standing in the way.

Verse 27: "Now you are the body of Christ and each one of you is a part of it. And in the church God has appointed first of all, apostles, second prophets, third teachers, then workers of miracles also those having gifts of healing. Those able to help others."

People recognize and confirm appointments, but God gives appointments. The word of God says, *"By their fruit, you will know them."*

THE FRUIT OF THE GIFTS

If God appoints, there should be the fruit of that appointment which can be readily recognized by anyone with spiritual perception. The minute you have to hang a sign outside your door declaring yourself to be an apostle you'd better ask yourself, if you were appointed or self-appointed?

You don't create a mango tree. You go outside and look at the fruit and you see that it is a mango tree. You don't get it mixed up with an orange tree at all. Why? Because of the fruit it produces. There should be fruit of appointment that must be evident.

Verse 29: "Are all apostles? Are all prophets? Are all teachers? Do all speak in tongues? Do all interpret? But eagerly desires the greater gifts."

I want us to make note then of the benefits of a "Ministry of Helps" that is functioning. We see in verse 27 and 28:

"Now, you are the body of Christ and each one of you are a part of his and in the church God has appointed..."

One of the **first** benefits is that we begin to get an understanding of the importance of <u>everyone</u> in the Body of Christ. Soon, those in the Body of Christ begin to realize that they are important to the overall function of the Body. One of the principles we see in Genesis is that God put inside of everything He created, the ability to reproduce. Therefore, everyone in the Body of Christ is important because they have producing potentials placed within them by the Lord.

Now, whether you utilize what God gives is another matter. You may misuse your gifts, but what God intended is still within you. Don't let anyone mislead you. God has put inside of you everything you need to function in the Body of Christ.

WE ARE DEPENDENT ON ONE ANOTHER

The **second** benefit is that we begin to understand the inter-relatedness of the Body of Christ. We will begin to realize that we are all dependent on each other. Immediately you have to deal with that "Lone Ranger" spirit that says, "I am the only one that is important." That doesn't work in the Body of Christ.

When people begin to function as the Body of Christ is supposed to, you begin to realize that you need your brothers and sisters. You have something they need and they have something that you need. Then we begin to encourage each other, pray for each other and build each other up.

Matthew 10:1 is interesting because Jesus, in His ministry, showed us some of these benefits.

He called his twelve disciples to him and gave them authority to drive out evil spirits and to heal every disease and sickness.

These are the names of the twelve apostles: first, Simon who is called Peter) and his brother Andrew; James son of Zebedee, and his brother John; Philip and Bartholomew; Thomas and Matthew the tax collector; James son of Alphaeus, and Thaddaeus; Simon the Zealot and Judas Iscariot, who betrayed him.

These twelve Jesus sent out with the following instructions:

Do not go among the Gentiles or enter any town of the Samaritans. Go rather to the lost sheep of Israel. As you go, preach this message: 'The kingdom of heaven is near.' Heal the sick, raise the dead, cleanse those who have leprosy, drive out demons. Freely you have received, freely give.

Do not take along any gold or silver or copper in your belts; take no bag for the journey, or extra tunic, or sandals or a staff; for the worker is worth his keep." Matthew 10:5, 7-10

The **third** benefit we see is, when a ministerial support staff functions as it is supposed to, we see the obvious expansion of the ministry.

Jesus could only be at one place at one time when He was on earth. He was limited to time and space. But He called these twelve and sent them out to expand the ministry. They were His support staff. So, a ministerial support staff that is functioning right causes the ministry to advance and the Kingdom to move forward. Because they are many, they are able to accomplish more than the pastor. Jesus sent them out to advance the Kingdom, to preach the gospel.

Have you ever wondered why some churches have stayed the same size for so long? They are not utilizing their support staff. The pastor is trying to do everything and doesn't want to delegate any authority; he doesn't want to train his people. And if he doesn't delegate jobs to his people, he is simply limiting his productivity.

In Matthew 14:13-21, we observe the **fourth** benefit.

When Jesus heard what had happened, he withdrew by boat privately to a solitary place. Hearing of this, the crowds followed him on foot from the towns. When Jesus landed and saw a large crowd, he had compassion on them and healed their sick. As evening approached, the disciples came to him and said, 'This is a remote place, and it's already getting late. Send the crowds away, so they can go to the villages and buy themselves some food.' Jesus replied, 'They do not need to go away. You give them something to eat.' 'We

**have here only five loaves of bread and two fish,'
they answered. 'Bring them here to me,' he said.
And he directed the people to sit down on the
grass. Taking the five loaves and the two fish and
looking up to heaven, he gave thanks and broke
the loaves. Then he gave them to the disciples,
and the disciples gave them to the people. They
all ate and were satisfied, and the disciples
picked up twelve basketfuls of broken pieces that
were left over. The number of those who ate was
about five thousand men, besides women and
children."**

When a ministerial support staff functions properly, not
only does the gospel go forth, but a multiplicity of needs
is met.

In the Old Testament, Jethro illustrated this same
principle when he advised Moses to organize.

UNDERSTANDING YOUR POSITION

In Acts, Chapter 6 we see another example of the
importance of people understanding their position and
responsibility. There are several lessons to be learned
from this passage:

1. As your church grows, the needs of the people will grow.

2. Every member of the church should be in their staff
   position in order to meet various needs of the church.

3. If the people ministering see themselves as "helps -
   volunteers," the job may not be accomplished for lack
   of commitment.

4. The apostles in the Book of Acts understood their
   calling and stayed in position.

5. When everyone stays in their position, more will be accomplished.

Some Ministers need to take note of Jesus' example. Jesus called the people together and organized them. Sometimes when people hear words like "organization" as it relates to the church, they get frightened. They are afraid because they think the Spirit will be grieved. No, the Spirit is going to be able to flow more freely.

Jesus organized the people so there could be some order and so that what needed to be accomplished could be done so much easier. He called them together, organized them, then He sent out the staff who fed the people in an organized way. Jesus had told them to make the men sit in groups of fifty to facilitate the feeding procedure. Jesus did not grieve the Holy Spirit.

A FUNCTIONING STAFF CAN MEET MORE NEEDS

When a ministry or a church has a staff which is functioning in their capacities, more needs can be met. If a need isn't being met in your church, it might be because you are out of position and not utilizing your gift. The responsibility of the leadership is to recognize your gift, train you and release you to go and do the work, to go and meet the needs.

Let's look at Matthew 8:23-27:

Then he got into the boat and his disciples followed him. Without warning, a furious storm came up on the lake, so that the waves swept over the boat. But Jesus was sleeping. The disciples went and woke him, saying, 'Lord, save us! We're going to drown!' He replied, 'You of little faith, why are you so afraid?' Then he got up and rebuked the winds and the waves, and it was completely calm.

The men were amazed and asked, 'What kind of man is this? Even the winds and the waves obey him!'

In this passage, the ministerial support staff here were the ones who manned the boat while Jesus slept. They enabled leadership to be preserved. Could you imagine if Jesus had to go in the boat and row too? He had just finished ministering to many people. Virtue was already out of Him and He was tired.

The **fifth** benefit of a ministerial support staff that is functioning right in the church, is that there be a preservation of leadership. Why is preservation of leadership important? Because the leader has the vision to lead, and to give direction and inspiration. If those who are supposed to follow are well rested and the leader isn't preserved, who is going to lead? Who is going to give direction? Jesus' staff members (His disciples) preserved Him for His next ministry.

EXERCISE YOUR FAITH

We see also in this same passage the **sixth** benefit - the opportunity for people to utilize their gifts. Now these men did not fulfill all of their responsibility. They did not exercise their faith when they had the opportunity. This point is vital.

A ministerial support staff should also exercise their faith in the midst of situations. If you have an area of responsibility in the church, you should use your faith, skill and initiative. Once the pastor has given some general guidelines, you should not have to run to the pastor for an answer to every situation. Allow the pastor to correct you and advise you later if need be, but at least do something.

The disciples didn't do anything. They saw the storm and woke Jesus up. I want you to notice something here. Jesus was upset. It's interesting. Jesus did not commend them that they did the responsible thing by waking Him from His sleep to deal with the turbulent situation. But instead He rebuked them! Why? Because they did not exercise their faith.

Why should He expect them to exercise their faith? Because they had seen Him utilize His faith over and over again. If they hadn't seen Him, then His comments would have been unfair to them. He told them, "You of little faith. Why are you so afraid?" Then He got up and rebuked the winds and the waves.

The **last** benefit of the functioning ministerial support staff is that you see the fulfillment of the vision God has given you. The vision that God will give a leader can only be fulfilled if a ministerial support staff is functioning in that ministry. I don't care how tremendous the vision looks, it will remain a vision without people. The vision requires people and I believe when God calls us into account, He is going to ask us how well we have fulfilled the vision of our local church.

When we begin to understand how important and vital it is for us to fulfill our part in the Body, in the local assembly and then in the greater Body, we begin to realize how true it is. We begin to realize why Paul used the analogy of the human body, because everything in your body was created to function with and for the rest of your body.

When you come to Christ, you are no longer your own. You gave up your rights but today everybody wants to hold on to their rights. Isn't that interesting? When you come into the Kingdom of God, you give up your rights to the King and your rights become His rights to use when and how He sees fit.

PRINCIPLES

1. People perish for lack of knowledge.

2. If you are going to be effective in the Body of Christ, you need to function in **your** parts.

3. People recognize and confirm appointments, but God gives appointments.

4. If God appoints, there should be the fruit of that appointment.

5. God placed within everything He created the ability to reproduce.

6. We are all related and dependent on each other.

3

MINISTERIAL SUPPORT STAFF

I refer to "Ministry of Helps" as support staff, because the word "help" brings images of volunteerism. You help if it's convenient, or with the attitude that you are doing someone a favor. Instead, we need to begin to think of ourselves as staff in the church.

If you are a staff member of an organization, you don't function if you want to, you function because that is your job. You function from an understanding that you are responsible. Our mind set must be changed and I think sometimes the very use of the word 'helps' has caused us to perceive a wrong concept of our role in the church.

I want you to start to think of yourself, not as helps only, but as staff. You are actually on staff. You're not just helping the pastor out or helping the church out. Helps may be your title, but your <u>function</u> is that of a staff member. You have the same responsibilities, and even more so, as regularly paid job.

For the most part, the job that you go to and where you are required to work so hard and diligently each day, is of a temporary nature. But when you are on staff in the Body of Christ, you are involved in something that is eternal. This is the big difference. If we are as diligent and faithful during the day, 9 to 5, how much more faithful should we be diligent about ministry work.

USE WHAT GOD HAS GIVEN YOU

In Luke 19, Jesus tells the parable about the talents. I read that for years and it always disturbed me. When I got to the end of the story, where he took the talent from the man with one, and gave it to the man with ten, I said, "For goodness sake, this is as unfair a story as I have ever read. God, how could you do that? That's unfair. I guess you know what you're doing, but it looks unfair to me." Then one day God helped me out. He said, "You need to understand the principle."

You don't give more to those who aren't doing anything with what they already have. Because then they will have even more to waste. You would have thought that the fellow that had the one, would have rejoiced and said, "Whew, I only have one, praise God! I don't have to worry about five, I'm going to maximize this one." No, the man sat down and said, "Well, I've only got one, and he has five, let him work." He decided to rest on his oars.

He missed it, and a lot of people in the Body are missing it. They're looking at someone who has five, and saying, "I have only one, so I'm not going to do anything." God is sitting by, saying, "But, brother, you could only handle one, you can't handle five. If I gave you five, you wouldn't know what to do. Also, your 'one' will take you a lifetime to maximize."

Now the "Ministry of Helps" has been referred to as a supportive ministry. In other words, the helps are holding up the hands of the leader. I have taught that principle myself, and I still agree with it. However, the "Ministry of Helps" is more than supportive. It is also <u>connective</u>. It is like a link in a chain, and everybody in the chain has a different job description.

In this chain, none is more important than the other. This connective role says that everyone is inter-related although their job descriptions are different.

The job description of the pastor is different from the ushers, and it must be respected as such. In one sense, his position is more important, but not more important the way the world thinks of it. In the Body of Christ, we're all equally important, but we respect and honor the position of the leader. He receives from God, and he has to give the direction. Yet everyone is a part of the "Ministry of Helps."

EVERYONE HAS A PART

In the broader picture, every believer is called to be a part of the "Ministry of Helps." Let's look at I Corinthians 12:27, "Now you are the Body of Christ, and each one of you is a part of it." In the church, God has appointed. The leadership or the pastor, recognizes, and confirms.

In every church, there's a member who feels that God has sent them to that church to keep the Pastor in line. I don't see this ministry in the Bible. God appoints, and the pastor recognizes and confirms the appointing of God. You don't walk up to the Pastor and say, "Hey Pastor, guess what? God has appointed me the prophet in the church". That is not Scriptural.

God sets up a leadership structure in the church, and God works through authority. God will not violate a principle that He Himself has established. God gives no one in the church, no committee or member, the ministry of correcting the pastor. God reserves that for Himself, and God gets very disturbed when you try to do His job.

Verse 27 says, *"God has appointed then, first of all, apostles, second, prophets, third, teachers, then workers of miracles, also those having gifts of healing and helps, those with gifts of administration, those speaking in different kinds of tongues."* Then in verse 31, Paul rebukes them, *"But eagerly desire the greater gifts."* The Greek translation is literally, "But you are eagerly desiring the greater gifts." It's a slap in the face.

Paul is saying, "I know you people, you're sitting around here talking about greater gifts, when there are no greater gifts. "Best gift" relates to the gift which is more appropriate at the time. We're all in the 'Ministry of Helps.'"

The prophet gives the word from God, the apostle blazes the way, the teacher teaches the word, the evangelist goes out and proclaims the word, particularly to the lost. We are all related and connected, and all of us have our function. All the gifts must operate in love.

The different gifts have been designed by God to cause his Kingdom to advance. In Genesis 1:28, God says to Adam and Eve, *"Fill the earth and subdue it. Be fruitful and multiply."* What were they going to fill the earth with? With men and women made in God's image and likeness, speaking like Him and in communion with Him. That's what God's still after, <u>the church filling the earth with Himself</u>.

A SUPERNATURAL MINISTRY

A part of the problem is that, as the Body of Christ, we fail to realize that the "Ministry of Helps" is supernatural. Notice that the gift of helps is listed with all of the other supernatural ministries. Everybody's ministry in the church is supernatural. Why? Because the work of the church is that of affecting the unseen realm. Our work is not natural. When people come through the doors of the church and the Word of God is proclaimed, it changes them. That's not a natural thing, something supernatural takes place.

Everyone in the team is involved in something supernatural. From the person at the door who greets the people, to the pastor who delivers the message, must all be in communion with God asking Him what the needs of the people are. "God give me a Word for them, tell me what they need tonight. Is it a word of encouragement? Do they just need a hug? Do they just need a smile? What do they need, so they can be in the position to receive from you today?"

You don't just stand at the door, and look pretty. You don't know who's coming through the door. It could be the next evangelist, who will reach your city for Christ. He doesn't look different from anybody else, but you welcome him.

The intercessors have been praying before the meeting, so the Holy Spirit could have access to the people. The musicians are in tune with God, and they know just where God is taking the service. The usher is responsible to maintain order, so he doesn't let anyone come in and disrupt. The janitor has done his job, he has kept the facility clean so it looks like a place you want to be in. With everyone working together and fulfilling their function, the stage is set for the Spirit to reach the hearts of those He chooses.

We need to have qualification for areas of ministry, so people can understand what they are doing.

Qualification in the world doesn't necessarily qualify one for a position in the church. We are after something supernatural in the church. We want to fill the earth with God, not with ourselves. No position is an end in itself, for each person is a part of a connective chain. You're part of a team where everyone is working for one Lord. We have one goal, and at the end of our service, we want the earth to be a little more full of God.

Since we are in this world, but not of it, we need to rely on God's supernatural ability to function. If the "Ministry of Helps" is to function in its full capacity, each worker must depend on God's help. This includes every area of ministry.

The vital connective and supportive nature of the "Ministry of Helps," is similar to that of various parts of the human body. The whole Body cannot accomplish its purpose without the cooperation of every other part of the Body. The moment one part of the Body decides that it doesn't need the others and is not going to cooperate, it has also made the decision to immobilize the Body. Unfortunately, there are those who have been doing just that.

VISION

The pastor, or the under-shepherd is responsible for the vision. It's his responsibility to seek God concerning the vision for the local expression of the Body of Christ. Every pastor should have a vision for his church. Without a vision, he's wasting time for he will have no sense of direction. It is like the blind leading the blind. If he doesn't know where he's going, how can the people know where they're going? It is called a ditch experience!

The leader is also responsible to write it down, and make it clear, so the people will know where the church is heading and run with the vision.

Now what does it mean to "run with it"? After the pastor gives you the vision, you're responsible to do your part in it. God isn't going to give him the vision to impart to you for you to sit there and say, "Oh, that's a nice vision. Pastor, are we really going to do that?" No, when the pastor gives you the vision, you're responsible to run with it. In other words, you're responsible to get to work not just to be busy, but to also be effective.

When the pastor shares the vision for the church in its infancy stage, that's when it's most difficult for you to see. But Habakkuk says, *"Wait for the vision, it will come"* (Habakkuk 2:2 (KJV). In other words, there's a progressive revelation of the vision, and it will come. Many of the things that are now a reality once existed as a vision of Bahamas Faith Ministries a long time ago. And we kept confessing it and as the vision progressed, it became a reality.

God operates by this principle, "Faithful over a little, ruler over much." If He sees that you can't handle a little, He isn't going to give you plenty. You've got to convince God that you can handle the little, then He's going to give you much.

If you have ten babies in the nursery department, and nobody wants to minister to them, why should God give you fifty? If you're not ministering to the thirty children in the children's church, how is God going to give you one hundred? If you can't love each other, and there's only one hundred fifty of you, how can you love a thousand? Think about it; God's not a wasteful God.

Many churches stand stagnant, because the pastor either has not given the vision, or he's failed to write it down, so that those whom God sends to the church, can find their place in it.

Now it's interesting that when God gives a pastor vision, there are those who sometimes become disgruntled and start leaving. Some people don't want to work and some don't want to be under authority. When it comes to these kind of people, if they decide to leave, thank God, wave good-bye and give them bus fare. All they were ever going to do is sow bad seed.

You need to be confident that if God tells you to start a ministry, He is responsible to see that the vision comes to pass. He will send the people and the resources you need.

The pastor has several responsibilities in relating the vision.

1. He is responsible to receive the vision from God.

2. He is responsible to interpret the vision.

3. He is responsible to communicate the vision to his people This means that he should write it down, or put it on an audio cassette, or both. I encourage pastors to provide the vision in written or audio form to every perspective member of his church, so that they can know where the church is going.

4. He is to insure that the Body has proper training in order to fulfill the vision. If we want to be good at what we do, we have to train our people. And it costs money to train people.

At Bahamas Faith Ministries we send our people to seminars. We pay either all or part of the cost, because we want them to recognize the importance of the information. Professionals pay for training which they feel will be beneficial to them and enhance their effectiveness. Why should the church not do the same?

Let me illustrate how I see Ministry of Helps operating:

**God calls, appoints, anoints and
gives vision to the leader.**

The leader transfers anointing and vision to people. The people accomplish the vision in an organized fashion and the Kingdom of God advances.

PRINCIPLES

1. "Helps" is the title, but staff is your function.

2. You don't give more to those who are not doing anything with what they have already.

3. The "Ministry of Helps" is supportive and connective.

4. We respect and honor the position of the leader.

5. Every believer is called to be a part of the "Ministry of Helps."

6. God will not violate a principle that He established.

7. The "Ministry of Helps" is a supernatural work.

8. Qualification in the world doesn't necessarily qualify one for a position in the church.

9. Be confident that if God has given you a vision, He will give you the resources to see that it comes to pass.

4

THE HUMAN FACTOR

There are two relationships that are important when you consider ministry. The relationship between God and man, and the relationship between man and man. Most of the time, difficulty does not lie with the relationship between God and man. The main difficulty lies in the relationship between man and man. If we are going to minister effectively, we have to come to terms with this relationship, or what I call the human factor.

A LIVING SACRIFICE

In Romans 12:1, Paul is talking to the church at Rome and he is preparing them for ministry. *"Therefore, I urge you, brothers, in view of God's mercy, to offer your bodies as living sacrifices, holy and pleasing to God—this is your spiritual act of worship."*

Now let's examine this verse a moment because it almost looks like there is a paradox here. He beseeches them to present their bodies as a living sacrifice. Now those two words seem to contradict each other. How could you be a sacrifice and yet be living? It almost sounds like Paul doesn't quite know what he is saying. But we know he does. He is saying that you must present yourself, with all of your faculties intact. This implies that contrary to what some may have been taught, God is not just interested in your spirit.

I know some people have taught that we should just be concerned about the spirit, "My brother, don't worry about the flesh." But Paul says to present not your dead bodies but living bodies.

You see, it is a little difficult for God to use you if the house that you are in is not functioning. It is like saying that you want to use somebody's car to transport people. The car is what you are going to transport them in; transporting them is what you want to do. But since you cannot achieve your goal without the car, you have to keep the car in shape. If you are going to minister, your physical body needs to be intact. It needs to be functioning properly, for it needs to be living.

Your physical body has its own agenda. I am sure many of you are aware of this. It wants to do certain things at certain times, and some of those things are not appropriate. So Paul says to present the body, —not just as a living body—but present it as a sacrifice.

Usually, when you think of a sacrifice you think of something that is dead. In a sense, this is correct. The reason he says to present it as a living sacrifice, is that there are some things you have to put to death. He is talking about <u>presenting your body under control</u>.

There are times when you might feel like you just want to go home. For example, you are supposed to lead the worship, and you complain that you don't feel like doing it for that time. But if you are going to minister effectively, you have got to present your body as a living sacrifice. You will have to be a person who is able to say to your body,

"Hold on, you are going to serve the purpose of God. And right now the purpose of God is to lead the people of God in worship you cannot therefore, go home now"

MINISTRY THINKING

So, first of all, Paul speaks of the physical body. Secondly, he speaks to their mind set. Some of you may have thought you just get up one day and you will be ready to minister. No, there is a preparation for ministry. Paul says, "Don't be conformed to this world." In other words, when you approach ministry in the church, even your thinking has to change.

The world has its own way of thinking about talents or abilities. There is a mind set that the world has that says, "The important thing is to be seen as many times as possible, and to be as popular as possible."

The thinking of the world is to compete all the time. Paul is saying, "Don't think this way." By this very warning, it is obviously possible for a tongue-talking, Bible-toting citizen of the Kingdom to still be conformed to the thinking of the world. Bear in mind that he was addressing the church not the unsaved. It is very possible for you to be a part of the church without changing your thinking.

If you are put in a ministry position with the thinking of the world, it is going to come out sooner or later. In order to do the will of God, you must think the way God thinks. Otherwise, you will not know the will of God when you see it. Your thought processes must undergo a conversion.

In Verse 3, Paul advises not to think of yourself more highly than you ought. Can you imagine someone in a ministry position and they think more of themselves than they ought? That means you won't be able to give such people any advice for they are unteachable.

Paul does not say that you are not important or that you are a nobody. What he says is that you should maintain a proper perspective of your importance. <u>You are important to the Body of Christ</u>.

Sometimes in ministry, when you occupy a position, without renewing your thinking, the enemy comes along and deceives you into thinking you are the only one who can do what you are doing. But, there is also someone who can do what you are doing better than you can. The reason you are important is that they cannot do it <u>like</u> you.

You should never become conceited. When God gives you a responsibility, if you are wise, you will report for duty diligently. You will say, "Lord, thank you. You have a spot for me and I am going to fill it. No one will get a chance at my spot."

EACH ONE IS UNIQUE

Psalm 139 says that God has a plan for you. If you correctly understand that, you will not worry about somebody else's position because you will appreciate the uniqueness of your own. You should be so busy trying to fulfill your responsibilities that you will not have time to look around and envy somebody else.

Sometimes, you may be tempted to look at others and say, "Wow, are they talented! I wish I could do all that." No, don't wish that. To whom much is given much is required. If God gave them much, God's going to require much from them. Personally, I have enough. I really don't want anybody else's talent or gift.

Paul says to think soberly, as God has dealt to each one a measure of faith (Romans 12:3). What does He mean by a measure of faith? Let's look at the context.

If God gives a measure of faith for you to function in your gift, and you take it upon yourself to try to function in somebody else's gift, who has to manufacture faith to do it? You. God stands on the side because that's not what He intended for you to do. This is usually when people end up faking it because God didn't give them that measure of faith.

Have you ever seen a situation in a church where someone gets up and gives a prophecy, and it is a little long? Someone else sits there and says, "Well, you know, I can give a long prophecy like that too." They wait until the next Sunday, and as soon as there is a pause, they go into action. After the first two words, everyone knows they are faking it. Why? They are trying to operate in somebody else's measure of faith. If you don't have the gift, leave it alone, don't fake it. I have known from experience, that people usually know when you are faking it. The best thing to do is to operate in your own gifts.

For as we have many members in one body, all the members do not have the same function. It is like two eyes trying to be two more feet. Imagine the picture. You end up with four feet, and you look monstrous. Think about it. Somebody trying to function in another person's gift is a frightening sight.

We have different gifts, according to the grace given us (Romans 12:6). You cannot judge where you are going by where you are. You may start out cleaning the church, but it doesn't say that is where God is going to let you end up. You have to start using the gift God gave you. I am not talking theory. I know what it is to clean the church, I know what it is to be an usher. You cannot judge where you are going by where you are now.

Some people have never used what they have, yet they want more. God doesn't operate that way. When God gives you something He expects you to use it. If you do, He will entrust you with more.

WE HAVE ALL WE NEED TO OPERATE

If you look closely at I Corinthians 12, you'll notice that God has given the church a complete package. God has placed in the church everything we will ever need. So, if it is prophecy, it is included. If you need teaching, it is there. If you need exaltation, there are those who can exhort. If you need leadership, we have leaders. If you need mercy He placed those who are particularly merciful there. God has put everything we need in the body. Yet, there is the problem.

Imagine someone who should be there to give exhortation, busy trying to prophecy. God put them there to give; that is to encourage. Instead of being an encourager, they are busy trying to be a prophet. Not only are they out of order, they are robbed of something necessary to help the body to function. God put everything in its place so that the body could function properly. So when you come to church, if you need a little exhortation, it is waiting for you.

In verse 9, Paul says, *"Let love be without hypocrisy."* Oh no, we don't have that in the church! That is in the world. Why would Paul write this to the church? If you understand the first part of the chapter, *"present your bodies as a living sacrifice,"* you'll recognize that love really has little to do with feelings. It is a decision you make to allow the love of God to flow through you. I am not going to wait until I <u>feel</u> like loving my brothers or sisters, because you might never feel like it. But you can do this only if you present your body as a sacrifice.

Do you understand why we have so many problems in the church? We have people who have never presented their bodies as living sacrifices. The body continues to tell them what it will do, how it will do it, and how long it will do it. The church is supposed to minister to people. But you can't minister to people if you don't love them, and you can't love until your fleshly desires are placed on the altar.

Verse 10 says we should *"be affectionate to one another with brotherly love, in honor giving preference to one another."* Now if we really do this thing right, the world will observe it and say, *"Look how those people love each other."* The world is supposed to be jealous if we function properly.

Now we know that you are not going to give any preference to anyone unless your mind has been transformed. If you have the mind of Christ, you will prefer others over yourself.

Verse 18 tells me that Paul encountered some human beings in his time. Have you ever met someone who is totally unreasonable? Anytime I meet someone like that, I ask God to give me grace. Paul says, *"As much as you are able, live peaceably with all men."* There are those with whom you cannot live peaceably, no matter how hard you try.

RENEW YOUR MIND

Why have we not been able, in some cases, to operate smoothly in our ministry areas? Because we are dealing with the human factor. The only way that we are going to be able to relate to each other, to work with each other, is if we have a renewed mind.

We can't have the mind set of the world because the world will tell us to try and compete. The mind set of the world will tell us that some positions are more important than others. In the Kingdom, no position is more important. Positions have different functions but they are all equally important. God will require of you an account of how well you fulfilled your position, not somebody else's.

Can you imagine wasting all of your life trying to operate in somebody else's gift and at the end of your life the Lord says, "How well did you do with what I gave you?" You reply, "But Lord, I was busy doing what Brother Joe was doing." The Lord says, "Hold on—I didn't ask you to do Brother Joe's work. I gave you your own gifts and talents and I expected you to fulfill your own responsibility."

I Cor. 15:1 says, *"We who are strong ought to bear with the failings of the weak and not to please ourselves."* We are talking about relating man to man. *"Each of us should please his neighbor for his good, to build him up."* Isn't that thinking different from the world? If I am busy building my brother up and he is busy building me up, everybody receives what they need.

God has a plan, if we are busy building each other up, together we are going to be strong, united and able to fill the earth with God's purpose. That is God's picture. Each of us should please his neighbor, for it is good to build him up. *"For even Christ did not please himself; but as it is written, 'The insults of those who insult you have fallen on me.'"* (Romans 15:3).

LOVE ONE ANOTHER

Verse 7, says, *"Accept one another, then as Christ has accepted you."* We need to understand that it is natural and normal that there will be things about your brothers and sisters that you do not like. It may be the attitudes, habits or mannerisms, but it is unscriptural to hold those things against them, and stop loving them as a result. All of us have character flaws which we are working on to improve. But Christ requires that we accept each other as we are.

Here is a beautiful principle. As you begin to love them and they can feel that genuine love, you may have opportunity to say, "My friend, I think you shouldn't say some of the things you say." They will know you are not picking on them or trying to be funny. But if you have concluded that you will neither love nor appreciate them, you'll never have an opportunity to help them. You have to accept people first. We like to wait for people to change before we accept them. That's not how God would have us behave.

It is the same thing in a marriage relationship. Many marriages are struggling because people don't understand His principle. They are waiting for their spouse to change. That spouse has been that way before you met them and they are going to be that way for a little longer until you learn to accept them just as they are. Then, through the changes you allow God to work in you, they can begin to grow.

We need to remember that God has given His precious "Ministry of Helps" to men and women with all of their imperfections. We must work together if we want to see His Kingdom come on earth.

PRINCIPLES

1. It is difficult for God to use you if your physical body is not functioning.

2. Present your body under control.

3. When it comes to the ministry in the church, your thinking has to change.

4. You should maintain a proper perspective of your importance.

5. You are important to the Body of Christ because no one else can do your work like you.

6. You cannot judge where you are going by where you are now.

7. Love has nothing to do with feelings, it is a decision you make.

8. In the Kingdom, no position is more important than another. They may have different functions, but they are all equally important.

9. All of us have character flaws we are working on.

5

AUTHORITY - GOD'S PLAN TO MAXIMIZE YOUR POTENTIAL

There is a major difficulty that pastors encounter when they seek to develop a vibrant "Ministry of Helps." It is a lack of understanding of the principle of authority. When we hear the word "authority," it immediately brings to our minds a very negative response. Why? Because we've only understood authority in a negative sense.

Authority is not a worldly concept, but a Biblical one that comes from God. God is the One who originated the whole concept of authority. Because of this negative response, instead of submitting to authority, most people run from it.

I know that authority has been misused and abused, I'm well aware of this fact. Buses and cars get into accidents, but we still use them. We continue to drive them, but we are careful to use them correctly. Because there are those who have abused authority, it doesn't warrant us throwing our hands up and refusing to be under authority anymore. Instead, we need to find out what the Bible says about authority, and submit to someone who is using it correctly.

A part of man's resistance to authority is the old rebellious nature, which originated with Adam. Rebellion is nothing new. If we understand Adam and Eve and why they were deceived, it will help us understand why people run from authority today. Let me explain this to you.

LIE OF SATAN

In the account of man's fall in Genesis Chapter 3, Satan convinced Eve of two basic lies. He convinced her that she would gain something that was good for her. And he convinced her that she would gain something she needed. The devil somehow convinced Eve that she needed to have what God said she couldn't have. To her dismay, and to all of our pain and suffering, she found out, after they had taken the fruit, that God wasn't keeping anything good from them.

The devil is always trying to convince us that what God tells us not to touch is something that we really need. Adam and Eve found out that what God was holding back from them was evil. Afterwards, they wished they hadn't eaten of the fruit, but, it was too late.

When people rebel against authority, it is for the same reason. They feel that the lines that are drawn are to keep them from something that they need. It's to keep them from something they have to have.

When you were a child and your parents said to you, "Don't go outside this yard," the first thing you wanted was to go outside the yard. Why? Because you thought "What are they keeping from me? It must be something good." As you got older, you realized that they were protecting you.

AUTHORITY IS INTENDED TO PROTECT YOU

One of the most powerful principles of authority is that it is <u>God's plan to protect you</u>. Don't ever forget that. It's crazy to think that God would create you in His image, and then restrict you unnecessarily. When God set up the boundaries in Eden, He did so to protect Adam and Eve.

According to Webster's Dictionary, authority is defined as, "1. An individual cited or appealed to as an expert. 2. Power to influence or command thought, opinion, or behavior. 3. Freedom granted by one in authority. 4. The person in command." We cannot discuss authority without defining power. According to Webster, power is, "the ability to act or produce and effect; power is energy, strength, force, and might."

We need to understand the relationship between power and authority. According to Psalm 62:11, we know who the source of all power is. "One thing God has spoken, two things have I heard: that you, O God, are strong..." We know that all power belongs to God. God is the Source of all power.

POWER VERSUS AUTHORITY

Power, in its simplest form, is the ability to do. Authority is the right to do it. You may have the power, but you might not have the authority. You may be a little more knowledgeable than the pastor in some areas, so technically, you may have the power. But you're not the pastor, so you don't have the authority or the right to do it.

There are six important facts about authority and power that I want you to understand.

1. All power is intended to operate under authority.

2. All authority comes from God. Who's the head of the church? God. Therefore, if anyone in the church has any authority, it has to come from God. All power is intended to operate under authority. When you go to the wall and you flick the switch, the current that runs through the wires is power under authority. If you don't believe me, put your hand in the wall and just hold on to the wires. Power, which is the ability to do something, is only useful when it is submitted to authority. Power on its own is unproductive and destructive.

3. Authority gives direction to power. This truth is clearly illustrated by our children. We are supposed to be giving direction to the energies of our children. If we let our children run wild, we are being irresponsible. God gave them to us, so that we could give direction to their energy and help them use their energy to fulfill a purpose.

4. Authority sets boundaries for power. It says, "This is the way we are going, and this is how we are going." Power, gifts, talents and abilities come from God, and He has a plan for them, hence He sets up the authority. Authority makes sure that you are not unproductive with your energies. We understand from Genesis 1, that gifts were given so that the earth could be full of His influence. He did not give them to us to make a name of ourselves. He gave it to us to fill the earth with His presence.

What do boundaries do? Some people don't understand boundaries, because they are negative. "They are to restrict me, to keep me in." No, they are trying to keep some things out. The boundary is to make sure that within limits, you can function to your fullest. Why? Because the authority knows that outside of this boundary, you cannot function.

Allow me to illustrate. When your children are small, you buy them a tricycle and say, "Ride in the driveway." Why don't you tell them, "You can ride in the street if you want to.?" Do you restrict them because you are trying to keep something from them? No, you are trying to preserve them. We need to recognize blessings when we see them. Authority and boundaries are a blessing.

5. Authority is God's plan to protect you. If you don't remember anything else, remember this. Imagine the children of Israel, with the soldiers behind them, and the Red sea in front. Moses prays to the Lord. God tells him to use the rod in his hand. He stretches it out, the sea opens up and he gives the command to move forward. What would have happened if the children of Israel had questioned Moses? I guarantee you, they wouldn't have been around too long. Authority is God's plan to protect you.

You may not always understand why authority does and says what it does. The disciples didn't always understand Jesus. I don't want you to think that they did, they were just like us. They were questioning Him and wondering all the time.

Sometimes, what the authority says doesn't seem to make sense, because the authority is giving direction from God. We wouldn't always know what God intends if we didn't have authority. You will not always understand them right away, but if you will obey, just like the disciples, you will understand in due time.

6. Authority is God's vehicle to enable you to maximize your ability and potential. It is within the framework of authority that everything God has given you can be groomed to its fullest potential. With this understanding, we can discuss principles of authority as it relates to the "Ministry of Helps."

PRINCIPLES OF AUTHORITY

1. All authority has to come from and be delegated by God. When authority is delegated to you, you are responsible to the person who gave you that authority. For example, you go on your job, and your manager promotes you, you become responsible to him. Why? Because he gave you that position of authority, He gave you his authority. So, when you speak to the rest of the staff, they have to obey you as if you were the manager.

There were some folks in the Old Testament, who did not understand this concept of authority. Miriam thought because she was Moses's sister, she could take certain liberties. She tried to usurp and rebel against Moses' authority. What she did not realize, was that Moses was under authority. He was not <u>the</u> authority, he was <u>under</u> God's authority. All he was doing was what he was told.

One of the few people in the New Testament who was commended, was the centurion. Do you know why? He understood authority. He said to Jesus, "Listen, you don't have to come to my house, I understand how this works. You do not have to be present, all you have to do is delegate." If the church would only understand this! We need to appreciate that all authority comes from God and is delegated by Him.

2. Where God sets you in the order of things is based on your purpose, and the goals that God has in mind for you.

3. Authority is actually designed to maximize power, not lessen or suppress it.

4. Power achieves its maximum fulfillment under the control and direction of authority.

5. All authority is delegated, and cannot be taken. This is very important! You may have power, and think you have authority. But authority is given to you, it cannot be taken by force. What do we call people who try to take national governing power by force? Dictators. Why? He was not given authority, he only had power. He misused this power to seize authority. Abuse of power, breeds abuse of authority.

We have people in the church who don't want to be under authority, and they try to tell the minister how to do things. And if the pastor does not listen, they decide to "do their own thing." He gets his little group together and moves on. I guarantee, it won't be long before someone in his little group does the same thing that he did. And it goes on and on.

6. You cannot be in authority, unless you have submitted to authority. The example of the centurion also stated this truth. How can you lead, when you don't know what it is to follow? And if you are wise, you will realize that if you don't know how to follow, when you are a leader, you won't know when people are following you.

God is a God of process, so don't try to skip any of the process. When you are operating with God, it is not like you operate in school. In some schools, after so long they get tired of looking at you. They say, "Look, you have got to go to the next grade." But that is not the way it is with God. You have got to go through every grade. There is no skipping your lessons. God's not going to make you a leader if you cannot follow.

Moses is a good example. When he killed the Egyptian, he thought he was ready to lead, but he wasn't. Because, when his countrymen taunted him, "Are you going to do to us what you did to that Egyptian?" he ran away. Does that sound like a leader to you? He hadn't learned all of his lessons.

What we need to learn from this is that desire is not enough. Moses had a desire to see his people free, but it wasn't enough. God put him in school until he was ready. When God sees that you are ready for authority, he will give it to you. In the meantime, just relax and grow.

7. We understand authority through submitting to authority. If you never submit to it, authority will stare you in the face and you won't recognize it. Position is based on purpose, not on importance as men view it. We respect the office of the pastor, because of his purpose. It is not that he thinks he is better than anybody for he is a man just like the rest of us.

Therefore, since God anoints different members of the body for various areas of ministry, if a member is not properly related to the leadership, he could find himself out of position. When God gives us anointing to function as a part of the expression of the Body of Christ, we find our greatest freedom when we know we are truly submitted to the local authority God has established.

PRINCIPLES

1. Authority is a Biblical concept that comes from God.

2. Rebellion is as old as Adam and Eve.

3. Authority and boundaries are God's plan to protect you.

4. God is the Source of all power.

5. Power is the ability to do. Authority is the right to do it.

6. Power is only useful when it is submitted to authority. On its own, it is destructive.

7. Boundaries make sure that within limits, you function at your fullest.

8. You can't skip any of God's intended process for your life and growth.

9. We respect the office of the pastor because of his purpose.

NOTES

6

ANOINTING - THE VITAL TRANSFER

One of the most important elements in the "Ministry of Helps," is the transfer of the anointing of the leader. When God gives a vision, He also gives the anointing or supernatural ability to accomplish that vision. I believe some of the failures we have seen in the operation of a vibrant "Ministry of Helps," is a failure to transfer the anointing of the vision.

DELEGATING RESPONSIBILITY

In Numbers 11:10-15, we see Moses expressing to God his frustration with his inability to accomplish what God had called him to do. I believe it is interesting to notice that God did not rebuke Moses, but instead gave him a solution to his problem. Moses' problem was the same as that of many pastors. He had a big vision, but too little human resources. So God instructed him to select seventy men of the "Elders of Israel."

I want you to note how he designated these men. He didn't choose the first seventy who raised their hands. No, *"The Lord said to Moses: 'Bring me seventy of Israel's elders who are known to you as leaders and officials among the people. Have them come to the Tent of Meeting, that they may stand there with you"* (Numbers 11:16).

In other words, not just any men. There was going to have to be some selectivity about who Moses should choose. They had to be elders and officers, who had the respect of the people.

God continues, *"I will come down and speak with you there, and I will take of the Spirit that is on you and put the Spirit on them. They will help you carry the burden of the people so that you will not have to carry it alone"* (vs 17). What does this mean? Why don't you just call them and let them go to work? There is an anointing that has to accompany a vision in order to ensure success. Academic or scholastic qualifications are not enough.

I want you to notice how God handled this. He did not say to Moses, "Call the seventy, and I'm going to anoint them." He said, "Moses, I gave the anointing for this vision, of bringing these people into the promised land, to you. You have the power and favor of God. I am not going to bypass the authority I have established. I will take the Spirit I gave you and give it to them."

We have people in the church, who believe they can bypass the authority that God has established. They believe God is going to give them a word for the direction of the church, that the pastor doesn't have. They come to the pastor and say, "You don't quite know what you're doing." No one in the church gives the pastor direction. He may ask you for some advice, counsel or recommendation, but his direction comes from God.

THE TRANSFER OF ANOINTING

God did not violate his own principle. He knew that in order for the seventy to serve properly, they needed to have the same spirit that Moses had. They needed the same understanding and supernatural ability. He had to give the seventy the same kind of spirit that Moses had because they were to assist him.

The transfer of the anointing that God gives is important if you are going to assist in the ministry. In our membership class at Bahamas Faith Ministries, we lay our hands on every member. Why? They must have the same anointing to do the work.

If God considered the act of transferal of the anointing from Moses to the people so important, I believe, in our churches it should be no less important. There are some lessons to be learned from this passage.

1. God always gives the initial vision and anointing.

2. In order to receive the anointing, there must be leadership qualities evident in your life. God did not ask Moses to simply bring him anybody, but God instructed Moses to look for leaders with specific qualities. In other words, their record spoke for itself. They had a good reputation among the people.

If you say you want to be a leader in the church, your pastor should be able to hand you a reference sheet and say, "Give this to one of your co-workers or your supervisor and let me hear what they think about you." They were also to be mature men who had balance in their lives.

3. You must have a heart for the people. You cannot minister to the people without a heart for them. You might not have it when God calls you initially, but if you allow it, He will give you a heart of compassion.

4. You are to be committed to the vision that the Lord gives the pastor. Don't come with your own agenda, instead be committed to the same vision as the pastor.

5. The anointing for a vision is the spiritual enablement and the spiritual understanding of the vision. Therefore, supportive staff needs the anointing to implement the vision.

6. In order for any vision to be fulfilled, each member of the Body must fulfill their responsibilities, purpose and maintain their position. Otherwise, the vision will not be preserved.

7. Without the support of the "Ministry of Helps," the vision will be limited by the physical constraints of the leader. The pastor can only do so much. He can't run the nursery, greet you at the door, play the piano, keep the church clean and deliver the message. With the assistance of the Body, the leader becomes unlimited in his outreach.

8. Without a utilization of the "Ministry of Helps," we are actually robbing the rest of the Body of the opportunity to develop to their full potential. Note that God never asked Moses to choose perfect men. Everybody can qualify. A leader is able to recognize potential in people. A leader doesn't choose perfect people; his job is to call gifts forth. You have not reached your potential, but a leader sees what you can become, and he pulls it out of you. God does the same thing. He looks at what you can become, not at what you are.

THE CHOOSING OF DEACONS

An example of these principles in operation is found in Acts 6:1, *"In those days when the number of disciples was increasing, the Grecian Jews among them complained against the Hebraic Jews because their widows were being overlooked in the daily distribution of food."*

The church was assisting the widows with provisions but it seems that the Greeks were being left out, while the Hebrews always seemed to have their needs met. So the Apostles met to try and figure out a solution to this problem.

Verse 2, *"So the Twelve gathered all the disciples together and said, 'It would not be right for us to neglect the ministry of the word of God in order to wait on tables.'"* They didn't say it wasn't important for the tables to be served. They just said it was not right for them to leave the Word of God to serve tables.

Verse 3, *"'Brothers, choose seven men from among you who are known to be full of the Spirit and wisdom. We will turn this responsibility over to them and will give our attention to prayer and the ministry of the word.'"* All they were looking for were men to distribute food. Why were they so concerned about these men being filled with the Holy Ghost when they were "only" serving food? Every ministry of the church is supernatural. The Pastor has to have people who are responsible to carry out his direction.

They were only serving tables, but they needed the same anointing, and the same heart for the people. They didn't need to be standing there distributing food and grumbling as they did it. They needed to have the same spirit as the leader. So they prayed for them and transferred the anointing upon them.

Here is the result of what happens when everybody in the Ministry of helps does their job. Verse 7, *"So the word of God spread. The number of disciples in Jerusalem increased rapidly, and a large number of priests became obedient to the faith."*

When the church works right, even some of the "dead heads" will start to get in line. Some of the "dead" churches will start to say, "Hey, we had better get ourselves together, and start working."

Their number increased greatly. Why? Because the pastor was free to hear from God, and God knew what the people needed. Because these men were able to hear from God and preach the word, needs were met, souls were saved, and the church exploded.

Note several facts about "helps" in the book of Acts. Number one, when the "helps" was added to the church, the Word of God increased. Every minister had to receive the anointing. The purpose of this was to give the men of God time to study the Word and pray. Stephen did mighty miracles because he proved himself faithful in serving. Church growth is a result of the work of the "Ministry of Helps." This example of the early church demonstrates that God will add to our church when He knows we can care for the people. I tell you again, God is not a wasteful God.

PRINCIPLES

1. When God gives a vision, He also gives the anointing or supernatural ability to accomplish that vision.

2. You cannot bypass the authority that God has established.

3. God always calls a man, not a committee.

4. A leader doesn't call perfect people. His job is to call gifts forth.

5. God will add to our church when He knows we can care for the people.

7

CONFIDENCE - A NECESSARY ATTRIBUTE

Many times, people are unable to function in their calling because they lack confidence. According to Webster, confidence is defined as, "the state of being certain." If you are not certain that God has a vital role for you to play in the Body of Christ, you cannot function wholeheartedly. Psalm 139 sheds some light on this important topic.

> **For you created my inmost being; you knit me together in my mother's womb. I praise you because I am fearfully and wonderfully made; your works are wonderful, I know that full well. My frame was not hidden from you when I was made in the secret place. When I was woven together in the depths of the earth, your eyes saw my unformed body. All the days ordained for me were written in your book before one of them came to be.** Psalms 139:13-16

KNOWING YOUR PURPOSE

When you understand that you have a specific role and function in the Body of Christ, several things happen.

1. Jealousy is eliminated. You don't have to be jealous of anybody's function or gift. Why? Because you have got your own. God put it in you even before you were born. When someone says, "I was born to do this," that's a true statement. Not only were you born to do it, you were designed by God to do it. When you begin to understand this, there is no more reason to be jealous of another person.

2. There is no need to envy. When you take your eyes off of what you call the "spectacular" gifts, and focus your attention on your function, you begin to understand that you are unique. With that uniqueness comes responsibility.

3. It will take away the worldly element of competition. It is a sad thing to see people in the Body of Christ competing against one another. Even worse than that, is to see a church competing against another church. We need to take extra care to guard against this tendency. We have been appointed, we need to get on with our appointment.

4. When you understand that you have been appointed, it does away with any inferiority complex. There are many people who feel inferior to others. If they could only get an understanding of the Word, a revelation of God's intention for them. Whatever appointment that Christ has given you, can relax and not feel inferior to anyone who has another appointment. We need to realize that God is the One who originated the whole concept of the Body of Christ. Everyone is valuable.

GOD'S PLAN FOR THE BODY OF CHRIST

God has a plan for the Body of Christ to function in a specific way. That is why He created us with different appointments. God intended for every individual to be functional in the church. He put inside everyone the means of achieving this function.

There are many churches that have failed to fulfill God's purpose for their existence, because they did not realize that they had the human resources sitting in their midst. Meanwhile, God has put inside these people gifts that are not being used.

We've got to begin to understand that all appointments have different responsibilities, yet are of equal importance. I think we have gotten mixed up and have allowed ourselves to revert back into the thinking of the world, where we judge function by importance. All the appointments have equal importance, but they have different responsibilities. We respect each appointment because of its <u>responsibility</u> in the Body, not because of its importance, for we all need each other.

Now let's look at I Corinthians 12:28. Here we see Paul listing the different appointments. *"God has appointed or set first of all apostles; second, prophets; third, teachers; and workers of miracles; also those having gifts of healing; those able to help others."* That includes everyone. We all are staff. That's right, you are not just helping out, you are staff.

If you think one is more important than the other, think about this. He said first of all, apostles. What is their function? They go ahead and blaze the trail, set the pace and give direction. The prophet comes along with the Word from the Lord. Thank God for him. But woe to the prophet if he doesn't fulfill his function, or to the apostle if he doesn't fulfill his function. Why? Because if the apostle, for example, does not move ahead, he is hindering the vision and those who should assist him. With appointments come responsibilities.

If the "Ministry of Helps" is to function in its full capacity, the persons set in the various positions must be dependent on God's help.

I am convinced that God had an even larger picture in mind, not just for the local church, but of the universal church. I believe that God places in His Body different gifts, not just for the functioning of a local assembly, but for the functioning of the church as a whole. If we could ever grasp that, we would change our nations.

Can you imagine if pastors begin to realize that, if they would work together we would change our nations overnight. When God thought of the church, God thought about a body working together and that's why we can't do it alone.

The vital, connective, and supportive role of the Ministry of Helps is similar to that of the various parts of the human body. The whole Body cannot accomplish its purpose without the cooperation of every other part, without the involvement of every other part, and every part is of equal importance in the Body of Christ. Should any one part of the Body decide it does not need the other parts, it has made a decision to immobilize itself and reduce its effectiveness.

Therefore, stand confident in the gifts God has given you. The Body needs you to be operating so our purpose can be accomplished.

PRINCIPLES

1 Not only were you born to fulfill a specific function in the Body of Christ, you were designed by God to do it.

2. There is no one who can function like you.

3. There is no wastage with God, everyone is valuable.

4. God intended and equipped every individual to be functional in the church.

5. If one moves forward, all move forward.

6. All appointments have equal importance, but they have different responsibilities.

7. God will judge each of us based on our faithfulness to His purpose, not the prestige of our titles.

8. Every area of ministry needs the anointing of God, not just the pastor.

NOTES

8

FAITHFULNESS - GOD'S PROMOTION PLAN

Promotion is a topic, I believe, that catches everyone's attention, because everybody wants to know how to be promoted. This principle will help you get promoted in the natural, as well as the Spiritual. We're talking about faithfulness as it relates to our positions in the Kingdom.

It seems like God has a way of coming back to us and asking what we have done with what He's given us. People like to talk about all the promises of God and His blessings, but, we also need to stop and ask ourselves, how faithful we have been with what He has given us? God has entrusted every one of us with gifts, and when God gives you something, rest assured, that God will come back to ask you what you are doing with it.

That really was the crux of what God was asking Adam in the very beginning, when He came and said, "Adam, where are you?" He was really saying, "Where are you in relationship to what I've given you? What have you done with it? Where are you in your plans and progress with it?"

Everyone of us, as citizens of the Kingdom, have been entrusted with the good news of the Gospel. We've been entrusted with the precious truths of the Word. We've been entrusted with the responsibility to see that the Word goes forth. And God puts us in a church so that the Word can go forth in an organized manner.

In the church, He puts us in different areas of responsibility. So, if we're to function, as our physical body functions, then we need to ensure that every member, every citizen, is in place and doing their part. Be faithful to what you've been called to.

Above all, God requires faithfulness from us. Intelligence is nice, and degrees are nice, but God is really after faithfulness. If you are talented and not faithful, what good is your talent? Keep in mind, if you are faithful, God has the ability to give you talent.

Andre Crouch is a case in point. According to his autobiography, his father prayed for the gift of music for him. They were was in a situation where there was no one to play the piano. There wasn't a music ministry in their church. When his father prayed for him, God gave Andre Crouch the gift of music. He has been playing ever since.

YOU SUPPLY FAITHFULNESS, GOD SUPPLIES THE REST

What God cannot supply is faithfulness, only you can supply that. God can give you talents and gifts, but He can't give you faithfulness. That is your part. You might be eloquent, but if you're not faithful, your eloquence doesn't matter. All the people in the Bible whom God used had to be faithful.

I want you to consider two words, "called" and "chosen." As the church, everybody's called, but being chosen is another matter. God would love to use everybody, but not everybody will present themselves to be used by God. God never has the opportunity to choose them, because they're not there when He's ready to choose.

In Matthew 20:16, *"So the last will be first and the first last; for many are called but few chosen."*

Webster's definition of being <u>called</u> is, "to be invited or summoned." An advertisement is a call, a personal invitation is to be chosen. <u>Chosen</u> means to be selected. Being called and being chosen is the difference between fulfilling all that God has created you to fulfill and simply being a part of the crowd.

Your faithfulness will determine your effectiveness and promotion in the Kingdom of God. Many times, men are promoted because of faithfulness; but unfortunately, they also promote because of favoritism. You don't have to worry about God doing that. God has one main criteria. He checks your faithfulness.

WHAT IS FAITHFULNESS?

According to Webster, faithfulness is, "firmly adhering to duty." It is being constant in performance, not just in attendance. It is to be consistent. In other words, you can count on that person to fulfill their responsibilities. You know they're going to be there. You know they're going to get the job done. You don't have to wonder about it. These words - dependable, reliable, consistent - should describe every Christian.

Faithfulness is the natural side of your ministry, and anointing is the supernatural side. So, God supplies the supernatural side, which is the anointing. But you have to supply the natural side, and that is faithfulness.

When both of those are in harmony, you have someone who is able to fulfill the purpose of God. You have someone who is always in place to receive the anointing, to fulfill their purpose. So the two of them have to come together. It doesn't make sense for God to give you anointing for what He's called you to do, although you're not there to use it when you're supposed to.

Sometimes people are not faithful, even in their daily responsibilities.   And it usually follows, if you're not faithful in your daily responsibilities, it carries over into the church. If you can't be faithful on your job, you will more than likely do the very same thing in the church, because we are creatures of habit.

You know that habits are difficult to break. Many times we need the intervention of God to help us break them. That's how strong habits are. You meet a fellow who's been drinking alcohol for 6 or 7 years and he wants to stop, but he hasn't found the help to break it.

Some of us have other habits, it doesn't have to be drugs or alcohol. If we are inconsistent in our daily activities, when you are born again and come into the church, nothing magical happens. You don't all of a sudden become faithful. So if you are a lazy unbeliever, and you get saved, you are a lazy believer. Salvation has to do with your spirit, but conversation has to do with your natural man.

GOD'S PRINCIPLES REMAIN THE SAME

I want you to understand something about how God operates. He operates by His principles and He doesn't change them because you think He should.

I have said that God does not promote in His Kingdom like men do in the world. In the world, men will change the rules of the game. But, in His Kingdom, God doesn't change His principles for anyone, regardless of who you are or who you know. God wants to help us with our natural responsibilities in order to prepare us for ministry responsibilities. If you can't be faithful with something that's in the natural, how are you going to be faithful with something that's eternal? That's the way God thinks and how He operates.

In Acts chapter 9, Saul was persecuting the church, and he was faithful in doing so. Now, I want you to consider this. Here was a man doing the exact opposite of what he should have been doing. In the natural, you would look at Paul and say that God could never use him. However, God saw the positive side of how this man could be faithful, if he could only understand what was right.

In Acts 9, Paul is called to service for the Lord. In chapter 13, he is being chosen. Between chapter 9 and chapter 13, 15 years passed. What do you think was happening to Paul during those 15 years? God was preparing him to be chosen. He was in preparation to function in his purpose. God gives each of us the opportunity to develop our faithfulness. Too often we have the impression that once we're called, we just step into the chosen path and keep moving. It doesn't work like that, we grow into our ministry.

God has one plan for promotion. It's called faithfulness.

PRINCIPLES

1. You can be talented and not faithful.

2. God cannot supply faithfulness, you must do that.

3. To be called is to be invited or summoned. To be chosen is to be selected.

4. Faithfulness is the natural side of your ministry and the anointing is the supernatural side.

5. Salvation has to do with your spirit. Conversion has to do with your natural man.

9

UNITY - THE NECESSARY CONNECTION

God has designed the Body of Christ in such a way, that it functions at its best and best fulfills its purpose when we cooperate with each other. The success of the church depends on the unity of the Body. The proper working of the "Ministry of Helps" depends on unity.

The word "unite" has a very interesting meaning. It means, "To put together, to form a single unit. (Webster). It doesn't necessarily mean that the individual properties that come together to form this single unit lose their uniqueness. That is very important. But to unite means that those individual properties come together to form a single unit. This best describes the Church. Individual members, every one unique in their own way, banding together to contribute to the success of the whole.

The Bible says that Christ is, "The Head of the Church." It didn't say He <u>was</u> the Church. He's the <u>Head</u> of the Church. When we come together, the Church then becomes visible, and it functions as it should.

THE CHURCH IN HARMONY

One definition of "unity" is, "a condition of harmony." That's a beautiful definition as it relates to the Church.

A musician would say that the music is in harmony when it is in tune, when it blends well. If it blends well, nothing is out of order. That's why musicians practice. The conductor wants to make sure that nobody is out of order.

He says to one over here, "A little lower." To the one over here, "A little higher," till everyone is in harmony. And when you hear the piece played correctly you say, "Oh, that's beautiful." Why? Because everything is in perfect order. That's a beautiful description of what God had in mind for the Church and how He intended for us to function.

We need to understand that God has put in each of us just what we need to function in the Body of Christ. Wherever He puts you, you have what you need to function there. The problem is, people are usually too busy just trying to get rather than trying to find out what they have to give. Part of that is due to lack of knowledge or wrong teaching. Many times, people have been taught that only certain ones in the Church are important, so you just go to church, praise the Lord and go home. But that's not what God had in mind.

Another definition of "unity" is, " a combination or ordering of parts in a literary or artistic production that constitutes a whole or promotes an undivided, total effect."

If we begin to understand that meaning of unity, we'll begin to understand that we are supposed to be producing "an undivided, total effect," that is, to move the Kingdom of God forward. That's all we're after, and what we should submit ourselves to do.

The final definition of "unity" is, "a totality of related parts."

UNITY PRECEDES PRODUCTIVENESS

In 1 Corinthians 1, Paul is writing to the Church at Corinth and we see that they had some interesting problems there. The devil knows that if a church doesn't have unity, there can be no productiveness, and I believe Paul realized that about the church at Corinth.

Paul, called to be an apostle of Christ Jesus by the will of God, and our other Sosthenes, to the church of God in Corinth, to those sanctified in Christ Jesus and called to be holy, together with all those everywhere who call on the name of our Lord Jesus Christ—their Lord and ours: Grace and peace to you from God our Father and the Lord Jesus Christ.

I always thank God for you because of his grace given you in Christ Jesus.

For in him you have been enriched in every way— in all your speaking and in all your knowledge— because our testimony about Christ was confirmed in you.

Therefore you do not lack any spiritual gift as you eagerly wait for our Lord Jesus Christ to be revealed. He will keep you strong to the end, so that you will be blameless on the day of our Lord Jesus Christ.

God, who has called you into fellowship with his Son Jesus Christ our Lord, is faithful.

I appeal to you, brothers, in the name of our Lord Jesus Christ, that all of you agree with one another ... 1 Corinthians 1:1-13

His desire is that they all, "speak the same thing." And that there be no, "divisions among you." That is, there would be no two vision among them. Why is it impossible for the church to move forward with duality of vision? It is simply because no one person can move a vision forward without everybody doing their part. We all have to be working for the same thing.

When you find a church like this, then you begin to see things happen. Have you known churches that were not moving forward? I guarantee that, part of the reason is that people were moving in different directions.

But Paul says, "...so that there may be no divisions among you and that you may be perfectly united in mind and thought.

"My brothers, some from Chloe's household have informed me that there are quarrels among you. What I mean is this: One of you says, 'I follow Paul'; another, 'I follow Apollos'; another, 'I follow Cephas'; still another, 'I follow Christ.'"
1 Corinthians 1:11-12

The point is, if you receive Christ, it doesn't matter who you received Him through. You are in the Body of Christ now, so let's get on with business.

Is Christ divided? Was Paul crucified for you? Were you baptized into the name of Paul?

This is what's called a spiritual spanking. These people were busy being contentious and the Kingdom could not advance. Paul found it necessary to rebuke them for that.

If God has given you a gift, then we should see the fruit of your gift. If the fruit of your gift is present, there should be some powerful things happening in your church. The Kingdom of God should be advancing in that assembly.

Paul continues in Chapter 3. He rebukes them for being carnally minded, thinking like the world. He goes on and gives them a picture of the Body of Christ and of the "Ministry of Helps" in operation. He says, "Look, here's how this thing works. I have planted, but it can't come to fruition just like that. Apollos comes alongside and waters. But who gave the increase? God is the source, men are only vessels."

He continues, "Look, don't get carried away. You've got your place and I've got my place, but the point is, if God doesn't bless everything, it's of no effect."

YOUR FAITHFULNESS, GOD'S BLESSING

You can utilize your gift, but if God doesn't come and bless what you're doing, it's useless. People sometimes utilize their gifts to show off and God will not bless it.

When people get hold of a dream, you can't stop them. The Wright Brothers decided they were going to fly. They had some failures in the beginning but they decided, "We're going to fly." And they didn't give up. If the church could grasp just this one truth, we could change the progress of the Kingdom.

Matthew 18:18, *"I tell you the truth, whatever you bind on earth will be bound in heaven, and whatever you loose on earth will be loosed in heaven. Again, I tell you that if two of you on earth agree about anything you ask for, it will be done for you by my Father in heaven. For where two or three come together in my name, there am I with them."*

Now the Lord wasn't really just talking here about church service, you know. That's not the only context in which this scripture should be interpreted. We usually apply this scripture to our speech, but I believe it is broader than that. How many of you know that you can say one thing with your mouth, but your actions can say something else?

We've been robbing ourselves. Whenever we gather together, two or three of us, we should be saying and doing things that reflect God's purpose. Let our actions start to do what our mouths agreed we would do.

In Acts 1:13, 14 we see a tremendous display of what unity can result in.

And when they were come in, they went up into an upper room, where abode both Peter, and James, and John, and Andrew, Philip, and Thomas, Bartholomew and Matthew, James the son of Alphaeus, and Simon Zealots, and Judas the brother of James. These all continued, in one accord....

In other words, they had one mind. Their attitude was, "Christ told us to wait here. We're going to wait here. We're going to pray." They had the same determination.

And when the day of Pentecost was fully come, they were all with one accord in one place. And suddenly there came a sound from heaven as of a rushing mighty wind and it filled all the house where they were sitting. Acts 2:1

Here's what I want you to understand, the day of Pentecost fully came <u>after</u> they had been in one accord.

RESULTS OF UNITY

I believe that we are going to see the Kingdom of God advance like it is supposed to, when we see churches where everyone is in one accord, in their place and doing their part. We haven't seen it yet. But I believe a day is coming when we will witness the real church in action.

Here are five results of unity.

1. Oneness of mind. Everyone is in agreement with the same thought.

2. Fulfillment of personal and corporate purpose.

3. People will really begin to see what the Church is like. Not until that orchestra is in perfect harmony can you fully appreciate the beauty of the orchestra. Until the Body is in total harmony with everyone in their place, can we really see the full manifestation of what God had in mind when he thought about the Church.

4. We will begin to see the power of God operating. Unity always produces power and productivity.

5. We will have a singleness of purpose. Not a magnification of our division, but a rejoicing in our unity.

We must understand this principle. For the Kingdom of God to advance, I must exercise the gifts God has given me and exercise them to the fullest, submitting to authority, prepared to receive God's anointing, confident in His gifts, faithful to use them and united with my brothers and sisters. Only then will we experience a full moving of the Holy Spirit and release of God's power.

PRINCIPLES

1. God reserves the right to give gifts as He wills, not as you will.

2. Do not be guilty of magnifying the gifts and missing the purpose.

3. God is the Source, man is merely the vessel.

4. Unity is the necessary connection in the Body of Christ.

10

ORGANIZING THE MINISTRY OF HELPS

The apostle Paul urged the Ephesian Christians to, *"be very careful, then, how you live—not as unwise but as wise, making the most of every opportunity, because the days are evil. Therefore do not be foolish, but understand what the Lord's will is"* Ephesians 5:15-17.

For many years, churches, Pastors and Christian leaders all over the world have been struggling to develop effective and supernatural churches, ministries and fellowships. It is easy to see that no one, as yet, has all the wisdom needed to complete the task, but God has given a measure of wisdom to the church to be effective in her mission. However, a common problem has always been the two extremes of no organization versus too much organization.

GOD'S FIRST PRINCIPLE - ORGANIZATION

What did God do when He observed a situation that was dark, confused, out of order, void of purpose, lacking a vision, or without a goal? His first move was to organize (Gen. 1:1-3). Before He created man He organized. Before

He made the animal He organized. Before He gave man dominion, He organized. God only gave authority after He had organized.

Organization is God's first Principle of life. He only creates His best after He has organized. He never changes and He remains the same today. If you want God's best, you must organize. Jesus reiterates this when He said, *"Whoever can be trusted with very little can also be trusted with much..."* (Luke 16:10).

The information on the following pages is intended as basic descriptions of the areas of responsibility, and will enable the pastor to become limitless in his ability to fulfill the vision.

Note: They are not in order of importance.

1. PASTOR AND HIS WIFE

(a) Study in the Word of God.
(b) Interpret the Word of God for the people.
(c) Pray for the Church.
(d) Discipline the Flock.
(e) Protect the Flock.
(f) Mobilize the Flock to do the work of the Ministry.
(g) Responsible for the flock and the vision.

2. ASSISTANT/ASSOCIATE PASTORS

(a) Responsible to assist Pastor and Wife.
(b) Assume authority and responsibility in the absence of the Pastor.
(c) Direct assistant to the Pastor in regards to pastoral duties and general oversight.
(d) Represent the Pastor at meetings.
(e) Co-ordinate the outreach ministries.
(f) Pray for the well being of the Church.

3. MINISTER OF MUSIC AND FINE ARTS DEPARTMENT

(a) Train worship teams and leaders.
(b) Responsible for all worship in the Church.
(c) Oversees all special music and dance ministry.
(d) Gives direction to the orchestra.
(e) Pray for the music and fine arts personnel.

4. DIRECTOR OF INTERCESSION

(a) Conduct regular intercession meetings.
(b) Organize strategic intercession for the leadership and ministry areas.
(c) Teach and train intercessors.
(d) Maintain constant communication with the Pastor.
(e) Pray for all the sick and any prayer requests.

5. ELDERS

(a) A spiritual aid to all the members of the church.
(b) Responsible for the aid to the widows, orphans, sick, poor and needy.
(c) Responsible for leading in outreach to jails, hospitals, old folks homes, new converts, etc.
(d) Pray for the members of the church.
(e) Assist the Pastor in the spiritual duties of the church.
(f) Assist in the direct oversight of the people.

6. YOUTH PASTOR

(a) Direct responsibility for the oversight of the youth.
(b) Responsible to pray for the youth.
(c) Responsible to develop and initiate programs and activities to benefit the youth and their parents.
(d) Train a team of youth ministers.
(e) Counsel the teens.
(f) Offer helpful information to the parents.

7. CHILDREN'S MINISTER

(a) Develop relevant children's programs and materials.
(b) Plan and organize children's ministry.
(c) Train a team of children's ministers.
(d) Pray for the children in the church.
(e) Responsible to assist in the spiritual growth of the children.
(f) Oversee children's church activities during adult meetings.

8. HEAD USHER/USHER

(a) Responsible to maintain order in the service.
(b) Assist people in being seated.
(c) Assist with prayer lines and altar ministry.
(d) Give information in regards to location of various departments.

9. HOSTESS

(a) Greet and welcome each person who comes.
(b) Issue church bulletins and other information.
(c) Give information.
(d) Pray for everyone who comes, to feel loved and welcomed.

10. HEAD DEACON/ DEACON

(a) Greet and welcome each person who comes.
(b) Issue church bulletins and other information.
(c) Give information.
(d) Pray for everyone who comes, to feel loved and welcomed.

11. HEAD OF SECURITY/ SECURITY

(a) Responsible for the personal safety of the pastoral staff.

(b) Ensure that the premises are secure at all times.
(c) Assist with any disturbances during or after meetings.
(d) Summon the Police and make necessary reports.
(e) May assist in transporting any special guests.

12. HEAD COUNSELOR/COUNSELOR

(a) Assist in altar ministry.
(b) Pray for new converts to come to Christ at each meeting.
(c) Have materials ready for altar response.
(d) Counsel and train other counselors.

13. SINGLES DIRECTOR(S)

(a) Direct oversight for the development of the singles.
(b) Conduct regular singles meeting and special seminars for teaching and fellowship.
(c) Develop a program for the single's ministry.
(d) Refer counselling to Elders when necessary.

14. AUDIO TECHNICIAN

(a) Responsible for the maintenance and security of all equipment.
(b) Ensure all machinery is ready for meetings.
(c) Set up, take down, transport and operate all equipment.
(d) Train a team of technicians.
(e) Pray over equipment.

15. CASSETTE MINISTRY DIRECTOR/TEAM

(a) Responsible to duplicate all cassette orders.
(b) Catalog and secure all masters.
(c) Develop methods of expanding the tape ministry.
(d) Pray that all taped messages bless the hearers.
(e) Train a team.

16. PUBLICATIONS

(a) Responsible for the professional display of all advertisements.

(b) Develop creative methods of informing the general public and other ministries of the resources available.

(c) Responsible to ensure information is properly communicated to the news media.

(d) Responsible for the overall public image of the ministry.

11

MANAGEMENT TOOLS

This chapter contains a number of management tools which will assist in offering some examples of the various forms and guidelines which will apply to all areas of Ministry of Helps. Feel free to adapt them to your individual needs.

1. Ministry and Planning Guidelines

This is designed to assist in the proper organizing and planning of each area of Ministry and should be completed by each Department Head. The Pastor should approve the overall plan before implementation. This document serves as the direction for the fulfillment of the Vision of each ministry.

2. Application for Ministry of Helps

This application or a variation of it should be completed by each applicant.

3. Reference Form
4. Report Form
5. General Guidelines- necessary general information
6. Codes of Conduct
7. Attitudes We Cannot Afford

Organizing and Planning Guidelines

1.   Name of Ministry

_____

_____

2.   Vision - Vision for this area of ministry

_____

_____

3. Purpose - Statement of Purpose

_____

4. Goals - Major Goals

_____

_____

5. Purpose - Objectives necessary to accomplish goals

_____

_____

6. Strategy - Methods of fulfilling objectives

_____

_____

7. Operation Plan - Plan of action

_____

_____

8. Short Range Plans

_____

_____

9. Long Range Plans

_____

_____

BAHAMAS FAITH MINISTRIES INTERNATIONAL

APPLICATION FOR MINISTRY OF HELPS STAFF

DATE: _____

NAME: _____ MALE _____ FEMALE_____

ADDRESS _____ P.O. BOX _____

TELEPHONE: (H) _____ (W) _____

ARE YOU BORN AGAIN? YES ☐ NO ☐ IF SO WHEN _____

ARE YOU FILLED WITH THE SPIRIT? YES ☐ NO ☐ IF SO WHEN _____

MEMBERSHIP STATUS ☐ OFFICIAL ☐ APPLIED FOR MEMBERSHIP

AREAS OF INTEREST

AUDIO ☐ TAPE ☐ RADIO ☐ T.V. ☐ BOOKSTORE ☐ ART ☐

PUBLICATION ☐ CLERICAL STAFF ☐ BUS MINISTRY ☐

NURSERY ☐ CHILDREN'S CHURCH ☐ HOST / HOSTESS ☐

STOREHOUSE ☐ MAINTENANCE CREW ☐ MUSIC MINISTRY ☐

COUNSELLING ☐ MISSIONS ☐ TEACHER ☐ YOUTH

MINISTRY ☐ SINGLES ☐ INTERCESSION ☐ TELEPHONE ☐

LIBRARY ☐ EVANGELISM ☐ DEACONS ☐ COMPUTER ☐

ACCOUNTS ☐ HOSPITALITY ☐

LIST ANY EXPERIENCE THAT YOU HAVE HAD:

_____

_____

LIST TIMES AND HOURS AVAILABLE:

MONDAY _____   TUESDAY _____

WEDNESDAY _____   THURSDAY _____

FRIDAY _____   SATURDAY _____

SUNDAY _____

USE THE SPACE TO INDICATE WHY YOU WOULD LIKE TO WORK IN THE AREA(S) YOU HAVE INDICATED:

(Hobbies, education, business etc.)

_____
_____
_____
_____

ARE YOU: YES   NO

1. Willing to take responsibility and make decisions?   ☐   ☐

2. Committed to do that which God has called you to do?   ☐   ☐

3. Willing to submit to the authority and follow
   directions of those whom God has placed in charge?   ☐   ☐

4. Willing to submit to the authority and follow
   directions of those that God has placed in charge?   ☐   ☐

Signature_____

Date_____

REFERENCE FORM

NOTE: This reference Form Must be Completed by a Regular Attender of _____
Meetings.

MINISTRY OF HELPS STAFF REFERENCE

_____ has made application with _____

_____ for the status of Ministry of Helps Staff and of

_____
Church

We endeavor to cultivate men and women of God, full of the Holy Spirit. who know their position and rights in Christ who aspire to create an atmosphere of faith where the Holy Spirit can minister. Your confidential evaluation of this applicant will be greatly appreciated.

Name _____ Profession _____

Address _____ How long at the above _____

Age _____ Telephone _____

How many years have you known the applicant? _____

Was your relationship: ( ) close   ( ) casual   ( ) business   ( ) family

PLEASE EVALUATE THIS APPLICANT IN THE FOLLOWING:

Spiritual responsibilities: ☐ poor ☐ average ☐ good ☐ excellent

Financial responsibilities: ☐ poor ☐ average ☐ good ☐ excellent

Business responsibilities: ☐ poor ☐ average ☐ good ☐ excellent

Financial responsibilities: ☐ poor ☐ average ☐ good ☐ excellent

Personal hygiene/ neatness: ☐ poor ☐ average ☐ good ☐ excellent

Ability to lead others: ☐ poor ☐ average ☐ good ☐ excellent

Is the applicants local reputation: ☐ good ☐ questionable ☐ bad ☐ unknown

Is the applicant's influence of others: ☐ negative ☐ positive

Comments: _____

Signature _____ Date _____

Ministry of Helps Report Form

Date: _____

Type of Meeting: Sunday Morning _____

                         Sunday Evening _____

                         Special Meeting _____

                         Mid-week Meeting _____

                         Other: _____

NUMBER OF STAFF PRESENT: _____

NAMES OF STAFF PRESENT:

_____   _____

_____   _____

_____   _____

LESSON OR ACTIVITY ENGAGED IN: _____

_____

GENERAL OBSERVATIONS: _____

_____

POINTS OF CONCERN: _____

_____

AREAS REQUIRING IMPROVEMENT: _____

_____

FOLLOW-UP NEEDED: _____

_____

OTHER COMMENTS: _____

_____

_____

SIGNATURE: _____

GENERAL GUIDELINES FOR MINISTRY OF HELPS

1. Time of Arrival:

(a) Sunday Morning Service	1 Hour before service for all Maintenance, Security and Technical Staff
	45 Minutes before service for all other Staff
(b) Sunday Evening Service	30 Minutes before service for all Staff
(c) Midweek Services	30 Minutes before service for all Staff

(d) Seminars/Conferences .... 1 Hour before service for all Staff

NOTE: If there is an emergency and you will be late, your Department Head should be informed. If you are not in position 15 minutes before meeting time, an explanation should be given to your Department Head.

2. Preparation Prior to Service

(a) Ensure necessary materials are in place.
(b) Note any special needs as they relate to your area.
(c) Prepare your area/distribute handouts.
(d) Check with your Department Head/Pastor for any special instructions.
(e) Read the weekly bulletin to be knowledgeable so you can assist.

3. Dress:

Sunday Services and Special Conferences and Seminars
Men: Jacket & Tie
Ladies: Dresses or Suits

Weekdays: Men - Shirt & Tie or Leisure Suit
               Women - Dresses or Skirt & Blouse

4. Personal Hygiene

(a) Cologne for men/ perfume for women (should not be overpowering)
(b) Clean breath (mints or freshener)
(c) Hair properly groomed

CODES OF CONDUCT

When an individual becomes an official, associate member of the church, he/she voluntarily accepts a unique way of life that seeks to provide development of spirit, mind and body to bring it into the mature image of the fullness of Christ. Each member is therefore expected to maintain the highest standards of behavior, performance and life style in keeping with Word of God.

The following codes are of mutual concern for the entire church family, administration, staff and members and should be faithfully committed to in the heart.

GENERAL:

a) Endeavor to do the will of God for my life and to exemplify Christ-like character, through my personal prayer life and study of the Word of God, and through faithful group worship.

b) Commit to yield my personality to the healing and maturing power of the Holy Spirit, and earnestly strive to manifest God's love toward my fellowman by following Christ's example to "do unto others as I would have them do unto me."

CONDUCT CODE:

a) There will be absolutely no smoking, drinking or use of illegal drugs by any member of the church. (I Corinthians 3:16)

b) No involvement in illicit sex or adultery. (Matthew 5:27, Luke 16:11 I Corinthians 6:13-18)

c) This church does not agree with nor condone cohabitation between unwed couples or any other

improper sexual relationship.
(I Corinthians 7:2, 10:8)

d) No involvement in usury or gambling.
(Habakkuk 2:4)

e) Maintain the highest standard of integrity, honesty
and morality. Cheating, falsification, stealing, or
other forms of dishonesty are expressly forbidden.
Immoral or indecent acts are expressly forbidden
(Romans 12:1-2)

f) Members may not frequent places of entertainment
or of a reputation which might bring discredit to
the ministry. (Romans 14:16)

APPEARANCE CODE:

a) The member must endeavor to present a good
appearance at all times appropriate to the occasion
and in harmony with good testimony of Christ.

b) Ladies may wear dresses, pant suits, skirts and
blouses, and other appropriate dress such as are in
harmony with a scriptural and effectual testimony
(modest apparel). I Timothy 2:9 I Peter 3:3

c) Men may wear suits, sports coats and ties, casual
shirts and any such dress appropriate to and in
harmony with a scriptural testimony.

SUGGESTIONS:

i) Beards and mustaches are acceptable but they
must be kept clean and well-groomed.

ii) Hair lengths on men must not be excessive, present
yourself as unto the Lord in the context of our
culture.

HYGIENIC CODE:

a) I Corinthians 3:16 - "Know ye not that your bodies are the temple of God and that the Spirit of God dwelleth in you."

b) Deuteronomy 23:10-14

i)   clean bodies

ii) fresh breath

iii) neat and clean clothing (as possible)

iv) hair groomed

These guidelines are not "thus saith the Lord," but they are in keeping with a good scriptural testimony.

ATTITUDES WE CANNOT AFFORD

There are certain attitudes and behaviours we cannot afford as believers. They include the following:

a) An unteachable spirit (Proverbs 3:11, 15:22,, 19:20).

b) Disrespect for others (Proverbs 14:21; 4:20).

c) Unsubmissive spirit.

d) Despising of spiritual gifts and the Word (Proverbs 13:13).

e) Envy, strife, a haughty spirit, hatred.

f) False witness (Proverbs 12:17,19).

g) Laziness (Proverbs 13:4; 19:15; 26:13-15).

h) **Pride** (Proverbs 13:10; 29:23).

i) **Unforgiveness** (Proverbs 18:19).

j) **Gossip** (Proverbs 17:9; 18:8,13; 26:20).

k) **Favoritism** (Proverbs 19:6).

l) **Fraud and dishonesty** (Proverbs 28:13,23).

m) **Impatience** (Proverbs 29:20).

LET'S STRIVE FOR EXCELLENCE TOGETHER THERE'S MUCH WORK TO BE DONE!

Five Principles of Leadership

①

Positively
Dover
June 28
10:00 — 8:00

Richard Pinder is available for speaking engagements and Seminars on Ministry of Helps and Church Growth.

Send letters and Inquiries to:

Richard Pinder
Bahamas Faith Ministries
P.O. Box N-9583
Nassau, Bahamas
!-809-393-7700

OTHER BOOKS FROM Pneuma Life Publishng

Beyond the Rivers of Ethiopia $6.95
by Dr. Mensa Otabil

Beyond the Rivers of Ethiopia is a powerful and revealing look into God's purpose for the Black Race. It gives scholastic yet simple answers to questions you have always had about the Black presence in the Bible.At the heart of this book is a challenge and call to the offspring of the Children of Africa both on the continent and throughout the world to come to grips with their true identity as they go Beyond the Rivers of Ethiopia.

Four Laws of Productivity $7.95
by Dr. Mensa Otabil

In Genesis 1:28, God commanded man to do four things: (1) "Be fruitful, and (2) multiply, and (3) replenish the earth, and (4) subdue it: and have dominion .." In the past, many people read and thought that this scripture only meant to have many children. This scriptural passage is not confined to reproduction, but is the foundation for all productivity. The Four Laws of Productivity by Dr. Mensa Otabil will show you how to: Discover God's gift in you, develop the gift, and how to be truly productive in life. The principles revealed in this timely book will radically change your life.

The 1993 Trial on the Curse of Ham $6.95
by Wayne Perryman

For the past 300 years, many Western and European Scholars of Christianity have claimed that Ham, Noah's third son, and his black descendants were cursed, and "[Blacks] would forever be servants to others." Over 450 people attended this trial. It was the first time in over 3000 years that Ham had an opportunity to tell his side of the story and explain exactly what took place in the tent of his father, Noah. The evidence submitted by the defense on behalf of Ham and his descendants was so powerful that it shocked the audience and stunned the jury. Evidence presented by the Defense was supported by over 442 biblical references.

Opening the Front Door of Your Church
by Dr. Leonard Lovett $7.95

A creative approach for small to medium churches who want to develop a more effective ministry. Did you know that 75% of churches in the United States have 150 attendance? Opening the Front Door of your Church is an insightful and creative approach to church development and expansion, especially for churches within the urban environment.
In this book Dr. Lovett... • Answers seven important questions that hold the key to maximizing effectiveness. • Explains the cost of following the Kingdom mandate. • Reveals how to open the front door while securing the sides and closing the back. • Illustrates Kingdom evangelization and liberation • Amplifies how your church can grow by being qualitatively oriented rather than numerically oriented. This book challenges those who want to

expand and develop their ministries to change their paradigms and live on the creative edge of God's future for His church.

The Flaming Sword $6.95
by Tai Ikomi
Scripture memorization and meditation bring tremendous spiritual power, however many Christians find it to be an uphill task. Committing Scriptures to memory will transform the mediocre Christian to a spiritual giant. This book will help you to become addicted to the powerful practice of scripture memorization and help you obtain the victory that you desire in every area of your life. The Flaming Sword is your pathway to spiritual growth and a more intimate relationship with God.

Another Look at Sex $4.95
by Charles Phillips

This book is undoubtedly a head turner and eye opener that will cause you to take another close look at sex. In this book, Charles Phillips openly addresses this seldom discussed subject and giver life-changing advice on sex to married couples and singles. If you have questions about sex, this is the book for you.

Strategies for Saving the Next Generation $4.95
by Dave Burrows
This book will teach you how to start and effectively operate a vibrant youth ministry. This book is filled with practical tips and insight gained over a number of years working with young people from the street to the parks to the church. Dave Burrows offers the reader vital information that will produce results if carefully considered and adapted. Excellent for Pastors and Youth Pastor as well as youth workers and those involved with youth ministry.

Talk to Me $5.95
by Dave Burrows
A guide for dialogue between parents and teens. This book focused on the life issues that face teens, ranging from drugs to sex to parents to music to peer pressure. This book will help both teenagers and parents gain a new understanding on these age old issues. Written "in your face" by a man who knows what it is to be a troubled youth living in a world of violence, drugs and street culture.

BOOKS BY Dr. Myles Munroe:

Becoming A Leader	**$9.95**
Becoming A Leader Workbook	**$7.95**
How to Transform Your Ideas into Reality	**$7.95**
Single, Married, Separated and Life After Divorce	**$7.95**
Understanding Your Potential	**$7.95**
Understanding Your Potential Workbook	**$6.00**

Releasing Your Potential   **$7.95**
The Pursuit of Purpose   **$7.95**

Mobilizing Human Resources $7.95
by Pastor Richard Pinder

Pastor Pinder gives an in-depth look at how to organize, motivate and deploy members of the body of Christ in a manner that produces maximum effect for your ministry. This book will assist you in organizing and motivating your 'troops' for effective and efficient ministry. It will also help the individual believer in recognizing their place in the body, using their God given abilities and talents to maximum effect.

The Minister's Topical Bible $14.95
by Derwin Stewart

The Minister's Topical Bible covers every aspect of the ministry providing quick and easy access to scriptures in a variety of ministry related topics. This handy reference tool can be effectively used in leadership training, counseling, teaching, sermon preparation and personal study.

Available at your Local Bookstore
or by contacting:

To Order or to receive a Free Brochure:

Pneuma Life Publishing
1-800-727-3218
1-805-837-2113
P.O. Box 10612, Bakersfield, CA 93389